FEB 1 5 2006

Complete Guide to Asset Protection Strategies

Mark Warda, Attorney at Law

GALT PRESS
a division of
Galt International, Inc.
Post Office Box 8
Clearwater, FL 33757
Tel: 727.581.8685
www.GaltPress.com

Copyright © 2003 Mark Warda, LLC

All rights reserved. No part of this book, except for brief passages in articles that refer to author and publisher may be reproduced without written permission of the publisher.

First Edition, 2003

ISBN 1-888699-03-5
Library of Congress Control Number 2003108045

Manufactured in the United States of America.

This publication is designed to provide accurate and authoritative information in regard to the subject matter covered. It is sold with the understanding that the publisher is not engaged in rendering legal, accounting, or other professional service. If legal advice or other professional assistance is required, the services of a competent professional person should be sought.
From a Declaration of Principles Jointly Adopted by a Committee of the American Bar Association and a Committee of Publishers

This product is not a substitute for legal advice.
Disclaimer required by Texas statutes

Published by Galt Press, Post Office Box 8, Clearwater, Florida 33757-0008. This publication is available by mail for $34.95 plus $4.30 Priority Mail postage plus Florida sales tax if applicable. For credit card orders call 727.581.8685 or fax 727.585.8423.

Table of Contents

Part One - Overview of Asset Protection Planning

Chapter 1   The Liability Crisis 9
Chapter 2   The Risks We Face 15
Chapter 3   What You Can Do to Protect Yourself 21
Chapter 4   What You Cannot Do to Protect Yourself ... 25
Chapter 5   Understanding the Asset Seizure System . 33
Chapter 6   The 5 Most Important Rules of Asset Protection   37
Chapter 7   The Costs of Asset Protection 41

Part Two - Shielding Yourself Against Claims

Chapter 8   Avoid Unnecessary Risks 43
Chapter 9   Get Enough Insurance 45
Chapter 10 Use Separate Legal Entities 47
Chapter 11 Carefully Word Your Contracts 55
Chapter 12 Insulate Yourself from Transactions 61
Chapter 13 Clean Your Financial Statement 65
Chapter 14 Protect Your Privacy 67

Part Three - Protecting Property in Your Name

Chapter 15 How Exemptions Work 85
Chapter 16 State Shopping 91
Chapter 17 Equity Stripping 93
Chapter 18 Future Acquisitions 95
Chapter 19 Homestead 97
Chapter 20 Tenancy by the Entireties 105
Chapter 21 Pensions and Retirement Accounts 113
Chapter 22 Wages 117
Chapter 23 Life Insurance 119
Chapter 24 Annuities 123
Chapter 25 Tools of Trade 129
Chapter 26 Personal Property 131
Chapter 27 Alimony and Child Support 133
Chapter 28 Public Benefits 135
Chapter 29 Other Exemptions 137

Part Four - Taking Property Out of Your Name

Chapter 30 Shifting Property: What's Legal/What's Not ... 139
Chapter 31 Making Gifts 143
Chapter 32 Limited Liability Companies 149
Chapter 33 General Partnerships 155
Chapter 34 Limited Partnerships 157
Chapter 35 Living Trusts 163
Chapter 36 Children's Trusts 165
Chapter 37 Charitable Remainder Trusts 169
Chapter 38 Domestic Asset Protection Trusts 171
Chapter 39 Offshore Asset Protection Trusts 175
Chapter 40 Business Trusts 187
Chapter 41 Nonprofit Corporations & Foundations ... 189

Part Five - When Disaster Strikes

Chapter 42 The Rules Change 193
Chapter 43 Attempting to Settle 197
Chapter 44 Bankruptcy 199
Chapter 45 Hiding Your Assets 207
Chapter 46 Hiding Yourself 211
Chapter 47 Enjoying Your Assets 217

Part Six - Your Immediate Action Plan

Chapter 48 Evaluate Your Exposure 219
Chapter 49 Get an Exemption Analysis 221
Chapter 50 Set up Your Plan 225
Chapter 51 A Final Word 231

Appendixes

Appendix A State by State Exemption Summaries 233
Appendix B Forms 239
    Form 1   Addendum to Contract-Arbitration
    Form 2   Employment Contract - 1
    Form 3   Employment Contract - 2
    Form 4   IRS Form SS-8 and instructions
    Form 5   Tenancy by the Entireties Assignment 1
    Form 6   Tenancy by the Entireties Assignment 2
    Form 7   State Law Worksheet

Index 253

Dedication
This book is dedicated to my wife,
Alexandra, who is my greatest asset.

Introduction

As a lawyer I read reports of new court cases every week. And the more cases I read the more frightened I became for my own financial well being.

A landlord took three days to fix a water heater and was liable for $775,000 in damages because a tenant was careless enough to boil a pot of water and spill it on her grandchild. A man earning $74,000 a year was ordered to pay $64,000 a year in alimony, child support and marital bills. A purchaser of a small piece of property was liable for hundreds of thousands of dollars in environmental cleanup costs.

Our legal system is obviously out of control and I was scared of becoming a victim of it. But as a lawyer I knew that the same system which could take everything from me could protect everything I own. That is the nature of law and always has been.

So I undertook the most detailed research I've ever done in my career. My entire life savings was at stake as was my future ability to retire and enjoy my final years. I read cases of people who were successful their whole lives and then lost their life savings at the age of 60 or 70. What is a person to do then, after a lifetime of hard work, live on social security in a small tenement, hoping not to be mugged by under-class thugs of the future?

I have read every book and article I could find on protecting assets. I wrote or phoned every expert I could find and asked questions. I wrote to hundreds of banks and trust companies in foreign countries to see what they had to offer. I analyzed all of this material and figured out which systems were the simplest, easiest and safest.

After protecting myself I still read every week of others whose lives are being ruined by outrageous lawsuits. So I decided to condense everything I have learned into this book in the hope that others can use it to protect themselves.

I know it is my fellow lawyers who are partly to blame for this crisis. Too many are pursuing ridiculous claims and pressing unfair arguments. So perhaps I can help with this book to make up for what they are doing.

This is not a book of theory. It is not a product thrown together because there might be a market for it. It is the material I researched for my own use, for protection from our crazy legal system. You can find no better legal device than one a lawyer uses for himself.

There is a lot of bad asset protection advice available on the market. With the Internet everyone with a couple hundred dollars is able to call himself an expert and sell his theories for thousands of dollars. This book will discuss the good as well as the bad, and the legal as well as the illegal. With all the information in front of you, you can decide which systems are best for yourself.

Part One - Overview of Asset Protection Planning

1   The Liability Crisis

It is not an exaggeration to say that there is a liability crisis in America. A few years ago a $3 million award for spilt coffee and a $4 million award for a repainted car were shocking. More recently juries have begun making $100 million and even billion dollar awards. Burglars are winning awards when they are hurt while committing crimes!

Since 1994 average jury awards have tripled to $1.2 million in all cases and to $3.5 million for medical malpractice.

Business owners are losing their life savings to people who hurt themselves through their own stupidity. Doctors are closing their practices because it isn't worth the risk. Whole industries are moving to other countries because they cannot afford the high cost of liability insurance.

This is not a partisan issue. People ranging from George McGovern on the left to Dan Quayle on the right have noted that the current system is in crisis, that it is crippling American businesses. Manufacturers of such items as football helmets and small aircraft have gone out of business because they could not afford the insurance to cover the outrageous judgments which juries in our nation are awarding.

America is different today. The American ethic used to be that if you worked hard you would eventually be well off. Today Americans believe that if you are lucky you will suddenly become rich. You can be lucky with a lottery ticket or you can be lucky enough to trip on someone else's property.

Television has shown people the life-style of the rich and famous and now everyone thinks he deserves to live the same way. People have forgotten that it takes work and perseverance to make it big. They have taken in an instant what it took another a lifetime to achieve.

Years ago people were only held liable if they were at fault for an injury. But a couple of decades ago some law professors and judges decided that injured people deserved compensation no matter who was at fault. They decided to make compensation of injured people a burden, not on society as a whole, but on the successful members of society. In a matter of decades they completely revolutionized the legal system without a single vote in any legislature. Such a rapid change was unheard of in the whole history of law.

In this new system billions of dollars are transferred each year from people who run businesses or own property to those who suffer injuries. But not all of the money goes to the victims. Lawyers siphon off up to 40% of most awards. No wonder they are fighting tooth and nail against tort reform.

The unsophisticated jury is their tool and they work their jury with precision, using juror profile psychologists, gory photographs and computer simulations. They work not with the law or the facts but with the emotions of the jurors. Of course the "victim" wins and whoever has the most money loses.

The system is like a lottery. Even if someone has a meritless claim there is a chance a sympathetic jury will award them a windfall. If they lose it costs them nothing.

The system is much more favorable to people filing suit than to people defending themselves. Attorneys will work for a contingent fee (no fee unless they win) for someone with a claim. In many cases attorneys spend tens, and even hundreds of thousands of dollars of their own money for "expert witnesses," investigations, computer simulations and other trial preparation to outwit the defendant. Once they win a case they have millions to use on preparation for the next case.

But to defend a suit one must pay an attorney by the hour as the work is done. And even if you win you have to pay your own attorney fees, which can amount to hundreds of thousands or even over a million dollars. Something is wrong when an innocent person can be financially wiped out by a frivolous claim, while the losing claimant suffers no loss.

In England the loser must pay the winner's attorney fees, so only serious claims are filed. But here there is no risk to bringing a weak or even false claim. It is so expensive to defend a suit that often innocent people pay a large settlement rather than pay twice as much in attorney fees to win.

England (and most other countries) forbid contingent fees for attorneys. In our system the lawyer agrees not to charge for his work unless he wins, but then he takes a big piece, often one-third to one-half of the entire amount awarded. Think of it, if a person is made a quadriplegic in an accident and a jury says he is entitled to millions of dollars compensation to last the rest of his life, should his lawyer get half of it for doing one year's work on the case?

The amounts of the verdicts are also getting out of hand. It is almost like play money the juries are giving away. Don't they realize that there are not unlimited piles of money to be given away? That each big award raises the price we all pay for insurance and products and services in society? For some dangerous products more than half of what you pay goes to insurance for those who will sue when they hurt themselves.

These are the kinds of awards juries are giving:

- Defamation of a former employee: $1.9 million
- Failing to diagnose skin cancer: $4.17 million
- Sponsoring a Christmas party where a guest later had a traffic accident: $5.87 million

Even if you have insurance it may not be enough to cover the kinds of awards juries are handing out today. For example:

- $41 million for a misdiagnosis of abdominal pain
- $49 million for a stillborn baby
- $77 million for giving an anti-asthma drug which caused the patient to become mute, blind and paralyzed.
- $84.5 million for children drowned and brain damaged in a swimming pool accident
- $569 million judgment against a lawyer for sexually abusing his son

Even people who have done nothing wrong are being held liable. It used to be that only people who were at fault were liable. Today whoever has money, the "deep pocket," is liable, no matter who was at fault. The courts are inventing new theories of liability to transfer money from those who have it to those who are "victims" of unfortunate accidents. Some examples are:

- $986,000 awarded to a woman who "lost her psychic powers" after a CAT scan
- $2.3 million awarded to a woman after radiation treatment for uterine cancer, including $1.2 million for "loss of life's pleasures"
- $300,000 for slapping a daughter twice on face
- $500,000 for causing emotional stress to wife in divorce
- $456,000 for letting a 27-year-old son drive a car, causing an accident
- $75,000 for spraying perfume on a person without permission

◆ $60,000 for cursing which caused "emotional distress"

A new type of law which has been passed in recent years in some states is a "product disparagement" law. This means that if you say something disparaging about, for example, Florida oranges, you could be sued. Suppose you find evidence that a new pesticide which has been sprayed on Florida oranges causes cancer. If you publicize this and it hurts the orange industry, you may be liable for millions in damages. What about freedom of speech? You might win the suit, if you can afford all of the legal fees to win both the case and the appeal.

If you want some inspiration in setting up an asset protection plan, look at the web site by Citizens Against Lawsuit Abuse (www.cala.com). It contains enough horror stories to scare you into an asset protection plan!

What has happened in this country? Has our success as a nation caused some people to become lazy, greedy and selfish? Is it natural for our system to break down and decay like the Roman Empire? Or is it something we can fix?

Whatever the reason we all do not have to be swept along with it. For nearly every law there is a legal loophole. That is how it has been for thousands of years. The Romans had lawyers who found them loopholes in the laws and the people in the middle ages did too. Lawyers write laws and other lawyers find ways to get around those laws. Lawyers change the laws and then other lawyers find ways around *those* laws. And one thing you can be sure of is that lawyers who are working for private citizens or for themselves are much more enterprising than those who would work for the government.

This book will explain to you the legal loopholes that you can use to protect your assets from an out of control legal system. In using legal loopholes to protect yourself from an unfair system you are following a fine tradition of people who have stood up for their individual rights throughout history.

There are some signs that asset protection is working. At least two law school professors have written articles warning that asset protection techniques must be stopped. One of their solutions is to impose criminal penalties for using asset protections and to put people in jail! (Interestingly the May 26, 2003 issue of The National law Journal reported that 74% of law school professors contribute money primarily to Democrats, who oppose reforming the tort system.)

2 The Risks We Face

The following is a summary of some of the most likely sources of liability which you may face. Some of them, such as loans you sign for, are under your control. Others, such as accidents or acts of your employees, are out of your control. Still others, such as slander or injuring someone, may only happen if you lose control.

Debts

- Business loans
- Personal loans
- Real estate loans
- Personal guarantees
- Alimony
- Child support
- Medical bills
- Legal bills
- Taxes

In most cases debts are under your control and can be kept reasonable. However, when combined with other unexpected liabilities they may overwhelm your ability to meet all of your obligations.

Alimony and child support are supposed to be reasonable, but there have been cases where these amounts have totaled 85% or more of a person's earnings. Medical and legal bills can strike without warning and can reach astronomical levels. Taxes should be simple to calculate but bad advice or a miscalculation can result in a surprise assessment along with interest and penalties.

In some states spouses are liable for each other's necessities such as food and medical care. This means you can be liable for your spouse's medical bills even if you do not sign a guaranty. In at least one state (Florida) the husband can be liable for his wife's necessities but a wife is not liable for her husband's necessities. The Florida Supreme Court said that this was not fair but that it was up to the legislature to change it!

Accidents

- ◆ Professional malpractice
- ◆ Auto accidents
- ◆ Homeowner accidents
- ◆ Rental property accidents
- ◆ Recreational vehicle accidents
- ◆ Sporting accidents

Accidents can happen without warning and wipe you out when you least expect it. On a Sunday outing a chiropractor accidentally drove his speedboat over a smaller boat which crossed in front of him, killing three teenagers. It cost him over a million dollars in legal fees just defending against manslaughter charges, even before he faced the civil liability. If you suddenly sneeze tomorrow while making a left turn and kill a pedestrian, will all of your assets be safe from a multi-million dollar lawsuit?

Legal violations and wrongful acts

- ◆ Environmental violations
- ◆ Civil rights violations
- ◆ Labor law violations
- ◆ Criminal violations
- ◆ Sexual harassment violations
- ◆ Slandering someone
- ◆ Inflicting violence on someone

Today there are so many laws it would be impossible for you to know all the ones which you must obey. But "ignorance of the law is no excuse" so you can be liable, even for criminal penalties, for an act you thought harmless.

Liability for Acts of Others

◆ Partners
◆ Employees
◆ Family members
◆ Those who use your vehicles

While the law considers you to have some control over the acts of others, in reality you have little control over much of what your employees or family members do. If your employee infects someone with AIDS, your partner commits malpractice or your child runs your car into a school bus, you may be held responsible.

And then there are potential liabilities which you probably couldn't even imagine. Did you know that if toxic chemicals flow underground from another property to under your back yard you may have to pay an unlimited amount to have it cleaned up? It may cost $100,000, $500,000 or even $1,000,000. And you cannot escape the liability by going bankrupt or giving the property away. The law in America today says that property owners are responsible for the cleanup of environmental hazards on their property no matter whose fault it is.

People have said that this is clearly not fair and that someone who is stuck with such liability should appeal the case. But people have appealed and they have lost. The courts have upheld such a system. Why? Congress has declared that pollution is a national crisis, it has realized that our government does not have the money to pay for it and has decided that sticking it to a few property owners is politically easier than raising taxes on the rest of the country.

One aspect of our legal system which is unusual is the doctrine of "joint and severable liability." Under this rule, **anyone** with **any** negligence in an incident can be liable for 100%

of the damages if the other parties cannot pay. For example, a woman was killed at Disney World while doing something she shouldn't have been doing. She was 79% at fault for the accident, her husband was 20% at fault and Disney World 1% at fault. But Disney World had to pay her husband damages for her death because it was the only one with money.

The fact is, in America today you can lose everything you have worked for in your life if you make one little mistake, or even if someone else makes a mistake and they do it on your property or can find some other reason to blame you.

But this same system which can take away your wealth can also protect it if you know the laws and the loopholes. This manual will explain in simple language each protection available to you and how to use it.

Divorce

While seeking to keep assets safe from creditors, you must not overlook the risk of divorce. Roughly half of first marriages and 75% of second marriages end in divorce. Some marriages clearly do not work from the beginning, but in many cases everything seems to be going fine and one party thinks that the relationship is great, but the other party suddenly feels that "something" is missing.

In setting up your asset protection plan, you should not disregard the risk of divorce. Putting everything in your spouse's name may protect it from creditors, but you would probably rather have them get it if your spouse runs off with someone else.

Loss of Purchasing Power

When the first edition of this book was published a very real risk appeared to be currency devaluation. The national debt was rising and an ever bigger portion of the income tax just covered the interest on the debt.

Since then the seemingly unthinkable happened, we have had budget surpluses due to a booming economy. And while the bubble has burst and the economy has cooled, interest rates are at record low levels and inflation appears dead. For the first time in decades deflation looks like a bigger problem.

But just when people least expect is when economic crises hit. (Which is why they become crises.) Most people buy stocks, gold and other investment when the prices are booming and sell out in despair when the markets crash, when they should do the opposite. Buy when the market crashes and everyone says they are poor investments, and sell when everyone is buying!

While the risks of inflation, currency crisis, and other economic turmoil seem nonexistent in today's deflationary environment, we should realize that the risks can return at any time. We live in uncertain times. We are presently at war against terrorism, and while we appear to be winning, a single act of flying a plane into a nuclear power plant or detonating a nuclear bomb in New York City could cause a financial crisis.

While we all hope and expect to prevail and prosper, we should keep our financial position flexible enough so as not to lose everything in case a crisis should occur.

Besides protecting your assets from lawsuits, you should also protect them from financial risks. Don't put all your capital on one type of investment. Stocks, bonds, real estate, gold and cash all offer different risks and rewards. You can invest in all of them through asset protection plans.

How Long Your Liability Can Last

For most incidents in modern life there is a relatively short "statute of limitations." This is the law that sets how long a person can wait before filing a lawsuit. For things like malpractice or liability on a contract it is between two and five years.

But for things like environmental pollution or lead paint poisoning, the limit for filing claims may be as much as twenty years after the event.

One big issue is when the time starts running. For contracts it is usually from when the breach (violation) of the contract took place. But for things like malpractice it can be from the date the claimant found out or should have found out he has a claim.

Thus, the time for filing a claim for an error in surgery could start running on the date of the surgery, or it might not start until five years later when the patient finds out that a pair of forceps was left inside her.

In one case a builder was liable for construction defects 31 years after he built some houses! This is because the owners did not discover the problem (that the houses were built on a cemetery) until that many years later.

This means that in some cases you cannot even retire and expect your liabilities are behind you. You may be hunted down in your retirement and if you are dead there may be lawsuits against your estate!

3 What You Can Do to Protect Yourself

The ultimate goal of asset protection planning is to set up your affairs so that no one can get your property. There are many simple ways to do this. In some states your home cannot be taken from you no matter what it is worth. In others, annuities, life insurance, or property owned jointly with a spouse may be untouchable. For more substantial interests a limited partnership or trust may be set up which is untouchable by even the most determined creditor. By knowing the rules and setting up your affairs accordingly you can own a substantial estate and have it totally free from claims of creditors.

This chapter summarizes what you can do to protect yourself, and later chapters explain in detail exactly how to do it.

Three Ways to Protect Your Assets

There are three main approaches to protecting your assets from those who wish to take them. The first is to keep the claims from reaching you. The second is to be sure that property you own in your name is immune from claims which do reach you. The third is to take property out of your name (but retain control). All of these methods can be used legally, and to be totally safe you must utilize all three approaches in your planning.

1. Keeping Claims from Reaching You

You can keep claims from reaching you by avoiding risky activities as often as possible, by conducting the risky activities you do have in separate entities such as corporations, by having enough insurance to pay for any claims that may arise against you personally, and by limiting your liability by contract.

Additionally, you can avoid being a target of lawsuits by keeping a low profile and not showing off your wealth. A huge home, expensive cars and furs may be fun to show off, but such a life-style may make you the target of someone who covets your wealth. Sure, it is fun to show off your success, but is the fun worth the higher risk of losing it?

Being conservative rather than boastful on your financial statements will also make you a less desirable target for lawsuits.

All of these methods of protecting yourself from suits are discussed in Part Two of this book (Chapters 8 - 14).

2. Keeping Your Property Insulated from Claims Which Reach You

Not all claims can be deflected so you must be sure that the assets you own cannot be reached by claims that do get through your first line of defense. Every state allows its citizens to own certain property which is exempt from the claims of creditors. In some states, such as Texas and Florida, you may have millions of dollars in property which cannot be touched by your creditors. In other states you may keep amounts ranging from a few thousand dollars to hundreds of thousands of dollars. The laws protect such things as equity in your home, pensions and annuities, insurance, tools, a car, and household goods.

All of the types of property which are exempt from creditors' claims are explained in Part Three of this book (Chapters 15 - 29). A summary for each state in Appendix A.

3. Taking Property Out of Your Name

Because most states only exempt limited amounts of property, most people need other ways to protect their wealth. And because creditors can only seize property owned by their debtor, taking property out of your name can make it untouchable by your creditors. However, there are strict rules covering how this can be done legally and what can get you into trouble. In fact, certain actions are criminal.

Some of the ways you can take property out of your name are to make gifts of it to your spouse, children or other relatives, or to convey it to a limited partnership or to a trust.

How to do this legally is explained in Part Four of this book (Chapters 30 - 41).

After You Have a Creditor

Once you know that a creditor has a claim against you your legal rights change. There are certain things which you can no longer do. At this point people often do desperate things, and these things get them into more trouble.

Your options after a creditor appears are discussed in Part Five of this book (chapters 42 - 47).

Your Action Plan

It is easy to read a book like this, to agree with it, and then to put it down and not take any action. Deciding which action to take and actually going through the steps takes a lot of effort. But asset protection is important to protecting the security of the rest of your life, and you should not procrastinate. Everything you have worked for your entire life can be lost if you are the defendant of a single lawsuit, even a frivolous one.

To make it easy for you, I have put together three different action plans. These are checklists you can follow step-by-step to protect your assets. Each one is more expensive and more complicated.

If you don't feel like doing much, you can just follow the easiest plan and keep the rules in mind when you make financial decisions in the future. If you really want to take action to protect yourself, you can follow the second or third plans. Each one costs a little mor in time and money but offers more protection.

If you take even a few of the steps you can be sure you have a few things left for yourself which cannot be touched should you be successfully sued. You can use these to start your life over if the worst happens.

The action plans are contained in Part Six of this book (Chapters 48-50).

The Best Protection

If someone offers you a foolproof or bulletproof asset protection plan, he is lying. There is no such thing. No one can know in advance how any legal situation will turn out.

One of the most valuable lessons of law school is that all law is almost always a gray area and you can never predict the outcome of a case. No matter how good your witnesses are and how many laws support your case, and how good your lawyer is, you can still lose.

The best you can do is to understand how a situation is analyzed and how to arrange your affairs to be the most secure. This book will help you learn what to do to put yourself in the most favorable situation if disaster strikes.

- ◆ A family or close relationship between the parties
- ◆ Little or nothing paid for the property
- ◆ Continued use or benefit by the debtor
- ◆ Secrecy of the transaction
- ◆ Debtor disappearing or leaving the area
- ◆ Financial condition of the debtor before and after the transfer
- ◆ A pattern of transactions after financial difficulties begins
- ◆ The general chronology of the transfers
- ◆ Transfer of all of one's property

Under the law, if even one of these badges is present the court might find that the transfer was illegal. If several are present it is even more likely the transfer will be found to be fraudulent.

Even if there is not found to be actual fraud, a court may find **constructive fraud** if certain factors exist. Constructive fraud is activity which legally amounts to fraud, even if there is not enough evidence to prove actual fraud. The factors which amount to constructive fraud are:

- ◆ The person is insolvent either before or after the transfer of property
- ◆ The person is left with an unreasonably low amount of capital after the transfer of property
- ◆ The person begins to incur debts beyond his or her ability to pay them as they come due.

The most important of these is whether or not the debtor is insolvent. In simple English, insolvency means that a person's debts exceed his assets. However, in court many factors are weighed in this determination.

For one thing, property which cannot be reached by creditors is not included in determining whether debts exceed assets. This would be exempt property such as a homestead and property in a trust outside of the country. Also, there is an important difference between the UFTA and the UFCA in this area. The UFCA finds fraud if the "probable liabilities" exceed the "present salable value" of the assets. But the UFTA finds fraud if the sum of "current debts" exceeds the "fair value" of the assets not including exempt property.

The difference here is that probable liabilities are usually much greater than current debts, and the present salable value of the assets is usually much less than their fair market value.

Example: If a person has assets of $1 million and debts of $500,000 he would appear to be solvent. But under the UFCA, if some of the assets include a partnership interest (which is not salable) and a vacant subdivision (which would be worth one-third as much when sold in bulk) then the person may actually be considered insolvent under the law.

By inflating the liabilities and discounting the assets the UFCA makes it more likely that a person will be guilty of fraud. But the UFCA has been replaced by the UFTA in many states. As of mid-2003 the UFTA has been adopted in the following states:

Alabama	Hawaii
Arizona	Idaho
Arkansas	Illinois
California	Indiana
Colorado	Iowa
Connecticut	Kansas
Delaware	Maine
District of Columbia	Massachusetts
Florida	Michigan
Georgia	Minnesota

Missouri	Oregon
Montana	Pennsylvania
Nebraska	Rhode Island
Nevada	South Dakota
New Hampshire	Texas
New Jersey	Utah
New Mexico	Vermont
North Carolina	Washington
North Dakota	West Virginia
Ohio	Wisconsin
Oklahoma	

It is pending in Mississippi and Tennessee. However, most states made revisions to the law and not all of them repealed all aspects of the UFCA.

The courts in some of the UFCA states (and the bankruptcy laws) allow persons to avoid some of the harsh results of this law. If an accountant using generally accepted accounting practices can testify that you are solvent, it is less likely that you would be found to be insolvent.

It is not necessary that a person obtain a judgment against you before you can be stopped from transferring your assets. Fraudulent transfer laws protect anyone who "has a claim" against you. These may include claims which are "unliquidated, contingent, unmatured disputed, undisputed, legal, equitable, secured or unsecured."

This means anything that you have done in the past, which could result in a possible claim some time in the future can be included. This shows the importance of taking action early.

Bankruptcy Law

Another law which determines whether your transfers of property are legal is the federal Bankruptcy Act. If you file for bankruptcy, the bankruptcy trustee is given title to all of your property, and if you previously made any transfers which were not legal, they can be set aside. This means that the trustee can get a court order requiring people who hold property which had been yours to return it.

Section 548 of the bankruptcy law states that any transfer of property within **one year of filing for bankruptcy** can be set aside. This law protects creditors of people who think that they can give all their property to their spouse and children and then file bankruptcy saying that they have no assets to pay their bills.

Under the law the bankruptcy trustee can order recipients of property to surrender it to him and can have the property seized if the recipient refuses to return it. If the recipient of the property has lost, damaged or destroyed it he or she can be held liable for the value of that property.

Section 544(b) of the bankruptcy law says that the bankruptcy trustee can use state law to determine if a transfer was fraudulent. This means that the UFTA and the UFCA adopted by the state in which the bankruptcy court is located can be used by the trustee to determine if a transfer was fraudulent.

Defense

A defense to a charge of fraudulent conveyance is that there was fair consideration paid for the property. This means that if you sold your expensive car to your son for a fair price, the transfer should not be considered fraudulent, even if you later spent the money on a trip to Europe.

Of course you need to have evidence of a defense. If you merely say you sold your car to your son and spent the money, you might not be believed. The court would want to know where your son got the money from and to see some proof that it was paid. Accurate bank records and receipts are required for a defense such as this.

Statutes of Limitations

As explained previously, a statute of limitations is a law which limits the time in which a suit can be brought. Fortunately, fraudulent transfer laws also have limitations. The UFTA requires that claims be brought within four years of the conveyance or two years after it was discovered or should have been discovered, whichever comes later. The statute of limitations under the UFCA varies by state. Under the bankruptcy law, transfers within one year prior to filing can be set aside. States (such as Delaware and Nevada) and countries (such as the Bahamas and the Cook Islands) which offer asset protection trusts have short and clearly worded statutes of limitations to limit creditor claims.

Nondischargeable Debts

Certain debts are not dischargeable in bankruptcy. This means that these debts will remain as claims against you until you pay them, and upon your death they will be claims against your estate. Nondischargeable debts can include the following:

- liabilities based upon fraud
- income taxes and excise taxes for the last three years
- alimony and child support
- liabilities for willful and malicious injuries
- liabilities from drunk driving
- government fines, penalties or forfeitures
- environmental fines
- student loans which matured less than seven years ago
- debts incurred with false statements
- debts which were nondischargeable in a previous bankruptcy
- credit card cash advances taken just before bankruptcy
- debts which were taken over by you in a divorce (if your ex-spouse objects)

Of course, if you have no property in your name, and there is no property in your estate at death, these debts do not have to be repaid. Some people are unaware that in the U.S. one's children do not have to pay one's debts. If a person dies with large debts and no property in their estate, in most cases the creditors are out of luck. By properly arranging your affairs you can assure that no property is in your name, but still have control of it during your life.

More specific rules about what can and cannot be done in exchanging nonexempt property for exempt property and out of your hands are contained in Chapters 15 and 30.

Further Research

For a web site with some valuable fraudulent transfer analysis, see: www.falc.com/transfers.htm

5 Understanding the Asset Seizure System

Before discussing the system for protecting assets it would help to understand how the system works when someone tries to collect money from you.

Someone claiming that you owe him money is a **claimant** who has a mere **claim** against you. Anyone whom you have injured is a potential claimant. If he files a lawsuit against you he becomes the **plaintiff** and you will be the **defendant**.

If he wins the suit the judge will sign a **judgment** against you, which is a declaration of what you legally owe the plaintiff. The plaintiff will then be your **creditor** and you will be his **debtor**.

There is no law forcing you to pay a judgment against you. Debtors' prison has been abolished and you cannot be jailed for failing to pay your debts. However, in some matters, such as failure to pay child support, you can be held in jail in **contempt of court** if a judge thinks you are intentionally disobeying a court order.

If there is a judgment against you, you can pay it voluntarily or your creditor can try to locate and seize any assets which are titled in your name. There are various procedures for seizing the assets of a debtor. **Garnishment** can be used to seize money held by a third party, such as a bank account held by a bank or wages held by an employer. In some states a judgment can be **docketed** with the sheriff. Then the sheriff can be instructed to **levy** on your property and sell it. The sheriff may levy by either seizing the property and putting it in storage or by posting a notice on or near the property that it is under the sheriff's control and cannot be moved.

To find out what property you own, the court can order you to attend a **deposition,** where you must answer questions about your financial affairs under oath. The creditor can **subpoena** your personal records such as tax returns, deeds, bank statements, cancelled checks, and so forth. If you fail to come to a deposition or to supply your records after being subpoenaed, you can be held in **contempt of court** and jailed. If you lie under oath you can be found guilty of **perjury**. If you bring falsified records you can be jailed for **fraud**.

Some of the property you own is **exempt** and may not be seized by a creditor. In most states a portion of the equity in your **homestead** is exempt. In some states you may own your property as **tenants by the entireties** with your spouse, and in some of those states such property may only be seized by creditors who have a judgment against both spouses.

You may take your property out of your name and transfer it to another entity, such as a **trust**, a **corporation,** a **limited liability company**, or a **limited partnership**. If the property is not in your name it usually cannot be seized unless the transfer was fraudulent.

A trust is an arrangement whereby one person, the **trustee**, holds property for another, the **beneficiary**. The person giving the property to the trustee is called the **grantor** or the **settlor**. The creditors of the trustee usually cannot reach the trust property because it is not the trustee's own property, he is merely holding it for others. The creditors of the beneficiaries, however, can often reach the beneficiaries' interest in the trust because they can seize the beneficiaries' interests, unless the trust is set us as a **spendthrift** trust. In a spendthrift trust a beneficiary cannot assign his interest and a creditor cannot seize it. But a person cannot set up a spendthrift trust for himself. More on trusts is explained in Chapters 35 through 40.

A corporation is a legal entity which is owned by its **shareholders** and run by its **officers** who are chosen by its **directors** (who are chosen by the shareholders). Personal creditors of the officers and directors usually cannot reach the property of the corporation because they are not owners of it, only employees. Creditors of a shareholder can seize the stock of the shareholder, and may or may not be able to reach the assets of the corporation. More on corporations is explained in Chapter 10.

A limited partnership is an arrangement between one or more **general partners** and one or more **limited partners** whereby the general partner controls the enterprise and incurs the liability and the limited partner puts up property hoping for future profits, but without further liability. Creditors of the partners can usually only have a **charging order** against the interests in the partnership and may not seize the partnership assets. This is explained in more detail in Chapter 34.

A limited liability company is like a limited partnership but where **all** the **members** have limited liability. In most states a limited liability company offers double asset protection, because members have no liability for company debts and the company assets cannot be taken to pay the members' individual debts. This is because creditors of an LLC member also only get a charging order. LLCs are explained in Chapter 32.

If you have a claim or a judgment against you and you give away your property or sell it for less than it is worth, that is considered a **fraudulent conveyance**. Such a transfer may be set aside by a court and the property may be seized by your creditors. If the person you transferred it to lost or destroyed it, he can be liable for its value.

If you have claims or judgments against you that you do not expect to be able to pay off, you can declare **bankruptcy**. **Chapter 7 bankruptcy** allows you to wipe out your debts and start over. You can wipe out all of your debts except certain kinds, such as student loans, alimony, child support, income taxes less than three years old, debts incurred through fraud or false statements, debts from drunk driving, government fines and penalties such as environmental cleanup, and willful and malicious injuries. In Chapter 7 bankruptcy you can keep all of your exempt property but you must surrender all of your non-exempt property. Filing Chapter 7 bankruptcy takes about 90 days and wipes out all of your debts except those listed above.

Chapter 13 bankruptcy is used by persons with less than $1,000,000 in debts to restructure their payments to allow them to pay them off over a longer period of time. **Chapter 11 bankruptcy** is similar but used by persons who have over $1,000,000 in debts. Often people try to restructure their debts under Chapter 13 then discover it is hopeless and switch to Chapter 7. This is euphemistically called **Chapter 20 bankruptcy**. More on bankruptcy is explained in Chapter 44 of this book.

6 The 5 Most Important Rules of Asset Protection

To successfully protect your assets from creditors you must follow five important rules.

1. Set up your asset protection plan as soon as possible

Once a suit has been filed against you it is too late to do most things which would best protect your assets. Even before a suit has been filed, but after you have committed an act which could give rise to a claim, it is too late to protect much of your property. To be completely safe you must set up your asset protection system before any possible claimant is known.

It is so easy to delay. You have never been sued. You might never be sued. Those millions of lawsuits filed each year are always against others. But each year, each day, the odds become greater that it is your turn to be handed those dreaded papers by the sheriff or process server.

But think about how your life would change if that day did come, if you got sued over some minor incident and lost most of what you have worked for. Think of the things you didn't buy to save money. The nights you worked late. All that can go to pay for new cars for a lawyer and his ne'er-do-well client, and more lawsuits against other innocent people.

2. Learn what your state's current exemptions are

The easiest asset protections you have are the state exemption laws. These are laws which protect certain of your property from creditors. In some states these can shield hundreds of thousands or even millions of dollars worth of property.

As explained in Chapter 49 you can get a detailed list of these exemptions in a book or on the Internet. But the laws are complicated and are subject to change both by the state legislatures and by court decisions. In some cases a minor detail on how the property is titled can make all the difference as to whether it is protected.

To be sure your property is set up correctly you should have a short consultation with an attorney who specializes in this area of law in your state. He or she will have read all the most recent laws and cases in your state and will be able to tell you what investments are safe.

Chapter 49 also explains how to find and work with an attorney.

3. Don't put all your eggs in one basket

Since law is a gray area and changes often, you can never know what will be completely successful in asset protection. Therefore, you should use several methods to protect your property. How to use trusts, corporations, limited liability companies, and other devices are discussed in this book. You should be using several of them and never put more than a small percentage of your assets in any one.

4. Review your plan often

The makeup of your property changes, the laws covering what is exempt change, and the risks in your life change. Therefore you must occasionally review your asset protection to be sure that all of your property is covered from all of the risks.

For example, as a young surgeon your greatest risk may be of malpractice, but years later you may face a greater risk of divorce or your teenagers having an accident in the family. Putting your assets in your spouse's name may protect you in the beginning but not later.

5. Don't look like the "bad guy"

I have read numerous court cases of people in lawsuits with creditors. In some the judge let them keep their property; in others they lost their property, even though the facts looked the same. Why? Judges have wide discretion in these cases and they can make a decision based on who appears to be the most honest and deserving.

If your actions make you look like a scoundrel who did everything to get out of paying a judgment, your asset protection plans will probably not work. But if you look honest and appear only to have acted prudently, to protect your family, you will be more likely to win.

If you lose an asset protection case it is not easy to appeal. Many people don't realize that appellate courts can only look at limited factors in a case. You aren't allowed to present your case again to an appellate court, or to find more evidence. The appellate court only looks at the file from the lower court and determines if any legal error was made based on what is in the file. So it is important to present your best possible case in your first appearances in court.

7 The Costs of Asset Protection

While some of the strategies in this manual for protecting your assets will be as simple as signing a bill of sale, other methods will involve some costs. There might be legal fees, service fees, lost interest or extra taxes. While some people cannot bear to get a quarter-percent less interest or to pay a dollar more in taxes, you must realize that these costs are insurance payments you are making to be sure you do not risk losing everything.

If you have never been sued or gotten into financial trouble it is easy to think that it will never happen to you and that asset protection costs are a waste of money. But your house has probably never burned down and yet you pay hundreds of dollars every year for fire insurance. Today you are probably much more likely to get sued than to have a fire in your home. The price you pay for asset protection may be all that it costs you to be sure you do not enter your golden years impoverished.

This extra cost can be compared to the risk/reward ratio of any investment. United States Treasury bonds pay much lower interest than junk bonds, but there is a much lower chance you will lose your money with treasury bonds. With asset protection techniques you may have a lower overall return on your investments, but you will be much safer and not worry about losing your life savings.

The amount you will pay to protect your assets will depend upon how great they are, how flexible you are in the type of assets you wish to hold, and the state you live in. Some states offer simple protections for many types of assets, while others offer few protections. In the latter you will need to be more creative in structuring your assets to obtain the most protection.

If you have substantial assets your best protection may be to move a portion of them overseas or to another state. Many Americans are worrying about the litigation crisis in this country and an asset protection industry has sprung up around the globe to help Americans protect our assets. Some may be scams, but others are safe, legitimate investments.

As with any type of investment you need to investigate asset protection products carefully. This book will give you an unbiased analysis of those techniques known to the author. Others you learn of should be investigated thoroughly. It won't do any good to take your assets out of the reach of your creditors if an asset protection promoter absconds with them.

Part Two - Shielding Yourself Against Claims

8 Avoid Unnecessary Risks

As mentioned earlier in this manual, America has changed. Things which were harmless activities a few years ago are now fraught with risk. In this dangerous new world you must change your actions if you do not want to be the victim of the new liabilities.

It may seem sad, but it is now too risky to serve in some volunteer capacities. Driving the Cub Scouts on an outing, having a fund-raising meeting at your home or sponsoring a charitable event could result in millions of dollars in liability if someone is injured or killed. Example: A Boy Scout touch football game "quickly degenerated into a tackle game" and a 16-year-old broke his neck. Two volunteers at the outing were found to be negligent and a jury awarded $7.1 million to the boy. Fortunately, the national Boy Scouts organization was able to pay that judgment, but what about smaller organizations? And what about the volunteers' legal fees?

As explained in Chapter 2, even if you are only 1% responsible for an injury, you may be ordered to pay for a lifetime of damages. The more wealth you have the more likely you will be found guilty.

In one case several children were injured when they were playing with dynamite blasting caps. Of course, when the caps exploded there was no evidence left of who the manufacturer was, so the children's families didn't know who to sue. The court ruled that since they could not know which company to sue, all companies who made blasting caps must pay a proportionate share of the damages! Even the most careful companies, which had done nothing wrong, were found liable. The court did not require any proof of guilt or wrongdoing.

Even if you had nothing to do with the injury you could bear all the financial burden if you are the deep pocket. This is a complete reversal of hundreds of years of legal theory which said that only guilty parties must pay for injuries.

Serving on a board of directors of a corporation used to be an honor. Now it is just too risky unless they provide you with millions of dollars in insurance. Numerous million-dollar judgments have been entered against people who have served as directors.

Joining in with a friend or neighbor to buy a boat or piece of property may sound like a good deal, but again the risk may be greater than the reward. If you still want to do it, you should consider using a corporation or LLC as described in Chapter 10.

The author was once asked to join a shooting club that owns a piece of land used for target practice. However, the thought that some day every member might be required to pay for cleanup of tons of lead on the property (from all the spent bullets) made it just too risky.

Before you agree to participate in any venture, be sure to consider all of the potential risks involved. If adequate insurance is available, you would have more reason to agree, but avoiding risky involvements is the best option.

9 Get Enough Insurance

One simple way to protect yourself from liability is to buy insurance. However, in the current crisis insurance may be unreasonably priced or even impossible to get. For some products the insurance can be three times the cost of manufacturing the item. For medical specialists the premiums can be more than what they earn.

One problem with insurance is that it may not be enough, no matter how much you get. A small unforeseen accident may result in a multi-million-dollar award. Several years ago a judgment over a million dollars was a rarity. Today there are hundreds of such awards each year, and $10 million and $100 million awards are not rare. With so many judgments now over a million dollars it is foolish for anyone with assets to have insurance policies with the usual limits of $100,000 or $300,000. For the cost of only a couple hundred dollars a year it is usually possible to get an umbrella policy which covers your home, vehicles and rental properties for one to five million dollars or more. Those with large amounts of assets should get an umbrella policy with $5 million in coverage, but keep in mind that even that may not be enough protection.

While insurance can protect against liability it can also attract lawsuits. Lately some doctors and other professionals have decided to go without insurance to deter patients and clients from filing lawsuits. For those with few assets or well-protected assets this may be an option.

However, in some states lack of adequate insurance is considered in an insolvency analysis so that asset protection actions may be deemed fraudulent. In these states a law may allow creditors to take your exempt assets if you do not have enough insurance or other assets to cover the usual risks of the business you are in. In other states insurance may be required by law for some professions.

Another drawback of relying on insurance is that it does not cover all possible liabilities. Legal violations such as environmental liabilities or civil rights violations, intentional acts such as slander, and other liabilities such as alimony cannot be insured against. Also, there are the risks that your insurance will be dropped after a minor claim, that coverage will be denied for some reason, or that an insurance company will not be solvent enough to cover all claims. The natural disasters in recent years caused several companies to close and others to cancel policies. A future crisis could be even worse.

For the insurance you do have, you must be sure that the correct names and risks are listed. Depending on your business structure (corporate, partnership, etc.) you must arrange your insurance accordingly. If you are an employee you must be sure you are listed on your employer's policy. If you are an employer you must be sure the acts of all employees are covered. If you have partners you must be sure all are covered.

Be sure that all insurance arrangements are in writing. Don't rely on your agent's verbal assurance. If you ask if something is covered, ask him to mail or fax his answer. If he fails to do so, send him a certified letter restating your understanding. The friendliest agent may forget what he told you once you have a claim.

10 Use Separate Legal Entities

One way you can protect yourself from personal liability is by setting up your affairs in a way that will shield you from claims. For example, as an individual business owner you would be liable for accidents caused by your employees. But if your business was set up as a corporation you would not usually be personally liable for acts of employees.

From a personal liability standpoint sole proprietorships and general partnerships are the riskiest types of ventures. In either of these entities you could be personally liable if your employee had a traffic accident on the way to the post office for you, or if someone slipped on your floor. In a partnership you could be personally liable for the acts of your partners. For example, in an accounting firm, medical practice or legal practice, if one partner makes an error, all partners are liable. In one case, sexual harassment by one partner in a law firm resulted in a $7 million judgment against the firm for which all partners were fully liable.

You can protect against this type of liability by structuring your affairs to insulate yourself. Some entities used to insulate from liability include limited liability companies, corporations, limited partnerships, and trusts. Because in most states at least one of these entities can be set up easily and cheaply, most lawyers consider it foolish to do business as a proprietor or partnership.

This chapter discusses ways in which these entities can be used to shield you from liability. With this method, the business entity incurs all the liability and there are no claims against you personally. For this to be successful, the entity should have only a limited amount of assets, because these assets will be subject to the claims.

The entities described in this chapter can also be used in a different way. They can hold your valuable assets and protect them from claims against you personally. This method is discussed in more detail in Part Four of this book.

Corporations

A corporation is one of the oldest and best shelters from liability. The purpose of a corporation is to let people put a limited amount of money into a risky venture and not worry about losing everything else they own. Corporations were invented hundreds of years ago to allow people to invest in exploration of the world. Before the corporation was allowed, investors in such ventures risked losing everything they owned if the venture failed, so most people were afraid to get involved. But with the corporation they could put only a limited sum at risk. If the ship returned home with gold they got rich, if it sank or was captured by pirates they only lost their initial investment.

Today the corporation can work the same way. It allows you to put up a limited amount of money in a new business and not lose anything else if the business fails.

For example, if a doctor sets up a medical practice in his own name then the doctor would be personally liable for all of the debts and liabilities of the business, such as rent, insurance premiums, supplies and even accidents caused by employees. However, if the doctor incorporated, the corporation would be considered a separate legal "person" liable for its own debts and employees. If all of the actions by the medical practice were taken in the name of the corporation, only the corporation would be liable, unless a liability were the direct result of an action done by the doctor. For example, if a nurse working for the doctor injured a patient and the injury resulted in a million-dollar judgment against the corporation, the doctor would lose whatever capital went into the corporation, but the doctor's other property and investments could not be touched.

One of the most famous cases used in law school involving corporate protection from liability occurred in New York. A man who owned hundreds of taxis put each one into a separate corporation and carried only the minimum insurance on each. When one taxi caused an accident the victim could collect the insurance on that taxi, and if that was not enough, could take the taxi itself, but could not touch any of the other taxis he owned which were in separate corporations. In a tough case in today's victim-wins society it is possible that a court would hold such an arrangement to be a sham, or against "public policy," but so far in most cases courts have not abandoned the protections afforded by corporations.

Some businesses need large amounts of equipment in order to conduct their operations. If the corporation owns a lot of expensive equipment, then all of those assets are at risk. To avoid putting the equipment at risk you could put it in a second corporation and lease it to the first corporation. If you wish to be even more creative you could put the expensive equipment in a "children's trust" and avoid taxes as well as liability. See Chapter 36.

One thing a corporation cannot protect you from is your own acts. If you personally injure a customer or patient, you can be personally liable for that, so a corporation cannot be your only protection. Also, if you agree to be liable for a corporate liability, for example by personally guaranteeing a corporate loan, it won't protect you. But it can protect you from other types of liabilities related to the business.

As an officer or director of a corporation you would have some day to day control of the activities of the corporation, and for this you could be liable, if you contributed to a damaging act.

In order to enjoy the protection of a corporation you must carefully follow the rules for corporations. Some of the most important ones are:

- ◆ Be sure that stock issued to you has been paid for
- ◆ Always hold annual meetings
- ◆ Never commingle corporate funds with your personal funds
- ◆ Keep accurate records and minutes
- ◆ Always use the correct corporate name with "Inc.," "Corp.," "P.A." or whatever is registered
- ◆ Always use your corporate title after your name
- ◆ Do not use corporate property for personal matters
- ◆ Have written agreements with yourself, employees and independent contractors

For asset protection purposes, you must also be sure that your corporation is not undercapitalized. This means that it must have a reasonable amount of capital for the type of business it is in. If your business needs few assets you do not have to have a lot of capital in the business, but if it uses a lot of capital equipment, you must have enough capital or your creditors may reach you personally.

To be sure of what is adequate capital, you should check with an accountant. Then record in the minutes the reasons for the amount of capital. Note that you made an assessment of the risks of the business and discussed the insurance needs of the business with an insurance agent. Be sure the debt ratio of the business is comparable with others in the industry.

Another important thing to consider is liability for federal withholding taxes. If a corporation fails to pay the required tax for its employees, the principal officers are personally liable for all amounts unpaid and there is an additional penalty of 100% of the tax which was not withheld. Withholding taxes should be one of the first items paid by a business.

Limited Liability Companies

The limited liability company (LLC) is a new type of business entity which was invented in the 1980s. It has the limited liability of a corporation with the tax advantages of a partnership. It has been compared to a limited partnership with no general partners.

In the relatively short time of fifteen years every state in the union passed a law allowing LLCs. There is a "model LLC law" which was written by a committee of legal experts and submitted to the states for approval, but most states made changes to the law before passing it. Thus, the LLC law of each state is different. In some states the LLC is very useful and inexpensive to set up. In others it is less useful and more expensive to set up. In the last few years states have begun to amend their laws to make the LLC even more useful. For example, in one great piece of legislation Florida eliminate the income tax on the LLC, allowed it to have just one member, lowered the fees and gave members double asset protection.

Basically an LLC is just like a corporation but you have less paperwork and in many states lower fees. After a short fight the IRS gave in on LLCs and agreed that an LLC can choose its own taxation, either as a pass through to the owners or as a separate entity. It can even allocate its profits and losses flexibly which makes it better than an S-Corporation.

The best thing about LLCs is that in most states they offer double asset protection. First, they offer protection from liabilities of the business just like corporations do, as explained in the previous section. But they can also protect your property from your own personal liabilities. If you personally harm someone, that person cannot get any of your property that you put into an LLC, if done properly.

Because LLCs have become so important to asset protection planning, they are discussed in their own chapter, Chapter 32, in this book.

Limited Partnerships

Some types of ventures, such as real estate projects, are often structured as limited partnerships. A limited partnership is a partnership between one or more general partners and one or more limited partners. The general partner is personally liable for all the debts and liabilities of the venture but the limited partners are only liable for the amount of money they contributed to the venture. It is also possible to use a corporation as the general partner thereby insulating everyone. However, unless the corporation was financially strong it would be difficult to get financing for such a venture, and there could also be tax problems.

Limited partnerships can be useful in two ways. By setting up a risky venture as a limited partnership you can limit your risk to the amount of capital you contribute. As a limited partner you would not be liable if the venture failed.

The other way a limited partnership can be useful is if you set one or more up to hold your other assets. Limited partnership assets cannot be taken to pay the debts of one partner, so if your assets are in a limited partnership your creditors cannot reach them. This is discussed in more detail in Chapter 34.

Trusts

A trust is an arrangement by which one person, the *trustee*, holds property for the benefit of another person, the *beneficiary*. A trust is set up by a *grantor* or *settlor* who conveys property to the trust. The trustee has no personal rights to the property but is legally obligated to hold it solely for the beneficiary. It is said that the trustee has a *fiduciary duty* to take care of the property and protect it for the beneficiary. Of course, the trustee is usually paid a fee to perform this duty.

While trusts are primarily known for their ability to avoid probate and the legal fees that go with probate, they can offer some protections from liability as well.

If real estate is owned by a **land trust** then liability on the financing can be limited to the assets in the trust. This is one way to obtain financing from a seller for which no one is personally liable. The way to do this is to set up a trust to buy the property you are interested in and have your trustee sign the mortgage and note (without personal liability on his part) which will be held by the seller. A third party lender and a sophisticated seller would require a personal guarantee, but if a contract is presented correctly this might not be requested.

Also, land trusts give you privacy by keeping your name off the real estate ownership records. You can own dozens of properties and no one could know. By keeping your real estate ownership private you make yourself a less likely target of law suits. Also, if your ownership of property is not disclosed you can avoid liability years later for lead paint or environmental problems. This is explained in Chapter 13.

However, land trusts do not protect against liability from other sources or for accidents or environmental problems on the property. For this many investors use an LLC as the beneficiary of their land trust. Land trusts cannot be used in all states, but an analysis of how they can be used in most states is contained in the author's book, *Land Trusts for Privacy & Profit*.

A **business trust**, like a limited partnership, can be used either to contain liability or to protect from liability. However, because business trusts are so seldom used and the law is not clear, it is better to use them to protect from liability than to contain liability, since corporations contain liability much more effectively. Using business trusts is discussed in Chapter 40.

Living trusts and **irrevocable trusts** are not usually useful in shielding you from claims and should not be used for this purpose. They are better used for shielding your assets from claims which reach you as explained in Chapters 35 through 39.

Tax Considerations

Most of the entities in this chapter which protect you from liability must file their own tax return and each has several options for taxation. You can usually choose the cash or accrual basis, you can adopt a fiscal year different from the calendar year, and in some cases you can choose between different methods of taxation. For example, a corporation may be taxed as a separate entity (C-corporation) or may pass its taxable income through to its shareholders (S-corporation). An LLC does not have to file a tax return if it has one member. Its income is reported on the owner's Schedule C.

To be sure to get the best advantages you should review the tax options with an accountant or tax attorney. Don't just ask them to decide what you should do. Let them explain the advantages of each choice and then you decide. Some tax advisors always do things one way because they haven't learned the other ways.

If you are pressed for time you may wish to put your trust in an advisor. However, there are several books available on corporations and the tax options available and you would be much better off if you understood how your business is structured.

Resources

See the last page of this book for publications explaining how to form corporations, limited liability companies and land trusts.

11 Carefully Word Your Contracts

Some types of liability can be guarded against with contracts. If you put into a contract exactly what you are offering to do, you should not be held liable if you do not accomplish more. For example, if you put in writing that an operation has 50% chance of success and it is not successful, there is less likelihood of a lawsuit than if nothing was in writing and the patient says you promised perfect results.

Arbitration Clauses

An arbitration clause should be used whenever possible. This is a clause which says that a dispute between the parties will be decided by an arbitrator, not a court. Why is this good? Because arbitration is faster and more straightforward than our court system. Court cases can be dragged out for years with all kinds of motions and investigations. And sympathetic juries can be swayed by emotional lawyers, bogus "experts," and slick presentations. Arbitrators can settle the case quickly and cut through the smoke put up by lawyers.

Here is a sample arbitration clause:

> Any conflicts between the parties to this agreement
> shall be settled by binding arbitration under the
> rules of the American Arbitration Association.

Be careful how the clause is worded. If it had just said "any conflict under this agreement," a person could argue that their dispute with you was not "under the agreement" so that arbitration did not apply.

Binding arbitration means that both parties agree to be legally bound by the arbitrator's decision. If the arbitration is not binding then the parties are free to start the fight over again in court if they lose in arbitration.

Mediation is similar to arbitration, but with a different legal meaning. With arbitration you ask an arbitrator to decide your case. In mediation, you ask a mediator to work with both sides to help them come to an agreement they can both live with. In cases where the differences are slight and the parties want a settlement, mediation can help. But in many cases the parties cannot possibly agree and mediation doesn't work.

In Appendix B of this book is an Addendum to Contract which you can use to add an arbitration clause to any contract you sign. Just be sure the other party signs it.

Jurisdiction Clauses

A jurisdiction clause is one which determines where a lawsuit between the parties can be filed. Being sued or filing suit far from where you live can be a lot more expensive than at your local courthouse. While you may not be able to change the clause in your contracts with large corporations, be sue to have one in any contracts you use for your business.

If you deal without contracts, you should put a jurisdiction clause on your invoices and order forms. Such a clause can be something like this:

> The venue for any action between the parties to this
> agreement shall be in Liberty County, Florida.

Business Contracts

In some lines of work, business is always handled on a handshake or a verbal agreement. This may work fine most of the time, especially if large sums of money are not involved. But at times there is not the same understanding by both sides as to what the agreement is and the dispute can end up in court. The hardest court cases are where there is no written evidence and all you have is the different stories by the different sides with no way to tell who is lying.

To protect yourself in any type of business you should have a standard contract that you give to all customers spelling out exactly what you are promising to provide and what your obligations are. This applies to all businesses whether you are a roofer, doctor, or an attorney.

This contract should be well thought out and should take into consideration everything possible that could go wrong. It should be in simple English rather than legalese. If there are any clauses which might be construed by a court as unfair or questionable, then there should be a place for the parties to initial next to them, signaling their clear agreement with each clause.

Employee Contracts

If you have employees you should have them sign employment contracts. These contracts can protect you from litigation and potential damages. Your employment contract should spell out what the employee's rights and obligations are, and it should make clear that the policy of your company is to forbid discrimination, sexual harassment, and other illegal activities. It should require them to report any offenses to you immediately so that you can take action.

As with other types of contracts, the most important clause to have in an employment contract is an arbitration clause. Arbitration clauses have been successful in protecting businesses from lawsuits under federal civil rights laws. The

U. S. Supreme Court has ruled that claims under the Age Discrimination in Employment Act could be made subject to binding arbitration. This would probably also apply to similar types of claims and could protect you from civil rights and sexual harassment suits. If not subject to binding arbitration, such suits could drag out for ten or more years and cost you a fortune in legal fees and lost productivity. A sample employment contract is included in Appendix B.

Independent Contractors

There are many advantages to using independent contractors rather than employees in your business. The most important have to do with liability and taxes. You are usually not liable for the acts of independent contractors with whom you contract. They are liable for their own acts and those of their employees.

As for taxation, you can avoid social security, medicare, unemployment and other taxes by hiring independent contractors rather than employees. However, the IRS is making a special effort to investigate companies which use independent contractors. There are penalties for incorrectly calling an employee an independent contractor.

Basically, if a person is in business for himself and has other customers he will most likely be considered an independent contractor. Also important is if he decides how and when the work will be done and supplies his own tools. If you have too much control over how the work is done, he may be considered an employee.

You cannot make an employee such as a secretary into an independent contractor because you usually have total control over this type of work. But if you give such work to a typing service that works at its own premises at its own hours, then you could consider it an independent contractor.

The IRS has a form, SS-8, which can be used to determine if a worker is an employee or an independent contractor. This is included in Appendix B of this book.

Marital and Premarital Agreements

A premarital agreement is a contract signed before marriage which spells out what will happen in the event of divorce or death of the parties. A marital agreement is one signed during the marriage. By signing such an agreement you can protect against a catastrophic divorce judgment or a lawsuit over your estate.

Especially in second marriages, premarital agreements are useful in protecting the rights of children born of a previous marriage.

Most people do not realize it, but everyone who gets married has a premarital agreement. It is the one contained in the divorce and probate laws of your state. Those who do not make their own agreement have one made up by the judges and the legislature. Naturally, one size does not fit all, and the distribution of your assets in the event of divorce may not be what either of you would prefer.

Not all premarital agreements hold up in court, but if both parties have attorneys, and there is a full disclosure between them, then the agreement should be binding. If the more wealthy party springs it by surprise an hour before the wedding with a threat to cancel the whole thing if it is not signed, then it probably would be thrown out by a judge.

With a marital agreement there is less flexibility than a premarital agreement. This is because upon marriage some rights already belong to the parties. Thus, in a marital agreement the parties would need to specifically give up some existing rights. For this reason it is usually necessary to fully disclose all of one's assets in order for the agreement to be legally binding.

Real Estate Contracts and Leases

Real estate deals are common sources of litigation. Since large sums of money are involved it is worth the time and money to hire an attorney and go to court if you have a good case.

Today the courts are expanding the liabilities of persons involved in real estate deals. In some states you are required by law to disclose "all known" defects in the property. In others you need only disclose "hidden" defects. If you do not or if you cannot prove that you made a proper disclosure then you may be sued for thousands of dollars in damages after the sale.

In addition, there are laws requiring the disclosure of such things as lead paint on the walls, radon gas in the ground, and even former military bases in the neighborhood.

If your contract or lease is drafted properly you can protect yourself from most kinds of suits. You should not expect a real estate agent to protect you completely in such a transaction. While some are very skillful and look out for their customer, many do not know all of the risks and some look out only for their commission.

Usually an attorney's fee is well worth the protection in putting together a real estate deal. While many deals may go through smoothly, if yours has a problem and you are not protected it could cost you thousands of dollars. Another alternative is a book which explains real estate contracts or leases. However, since laws change constantly, a book would not be able to keep up with the most recent changes.

Daily Contracts

Some people may consider it to be going too far but to be even more sure of avoiding litigation, some suggest that simple contract forms be used in everyday transactions.

For example, if you sell your used refrigerator in a garage sale, writing on the receipt that the item is sold "as is" with no warranties can protect you from a nuisance suit if it breaks down a week later.

Resources

See the last page of this book for a number of books containing useful contracts.

12 Insulate Yourself from Transactions

One way to protect yourself from liability is to distance yourself from the risky transaction. This can be done both in the sales transaction and the financing.

Selling Property

You can limit your risk of liability in selling property if you first sell to a "safe" party who then sells it to the general public.

For example, suppose you own a piece of property that has been owned for many years and want to sell it. Many real estate agents, to protect themselves from lawsuits and liability, have horrendous, detailed questionnaires for sellers. They as if there was *ever* a plumbing problem, *ever* a roof problem, *any* known neighborhood problem, *anything* that would affect the value of the property... etc. Why should a seller have to confess his lifetime experiences with the property? Shouldn't the buyer get his own inspector determine for himself what the property is worth to him?

Even if you disclose everything, and honestly don't know of any other problems with the property, if a problem arose right after the closing (such as the heater going out) the buyer could argue that you must have known, and therefore must have lied in the disclosure.

In some states, selling "as is" is not enough protection. You can still get sued if the buyer finds something seriously wrong with the property.

The best way to sell would be to sell to someone "safe" and let that party sell to the public. For example, if you sold the property to a corporation and the corporation shortly thereafter listed the property for sale, the corporation could honestly answer the disclosure statement by saying it never had a problem with the property and knew of no problems. Of course you could not form a one-man corporation yourself. But if you had a relative or friend who could do so, you would probably gain some protection. In some states corporations cost less than $100 to form so it might be worth forming one just for one transaction, though it could be useful for future transactions.

You might also find a safe buyer to sell to. One investor who needed to sell a property quickly sold it to the tenants and held a mortgage. The tenants then put the property on the market, sold it to a new party several months later and left the state. Although the new buyer assumed the mortgage, he could not blame the investor for any problems on the property. His only recourse was against the former tenant who couldn't be found.

Financing a Sale

One legal protection that can provide you with asset protection is the concept of a "holder in due course." This is a person who buys a financing instrument from someone else. The law is that if you buy something with financing through the seller, and the seller sells the obligation, you cannot use any arguments about defects in the product against the holder of the obligation.

A common use of this law is when used car companies hold the financing when they sell the cars, but then immediately sell the note to another company. The buyers can't stop paying if the cars go bad, because they are now paying a third, unrelated party which has no responsibility for the condition of the car. The buyer can sue the car dealer, but they can't stop making the payments.

This law has been abused by dealers who knowingly sell defective products and courts have refused to enforce this law where the third party finance company was related to the dishonest dealer or knew what the dealer was doing. But in general this law works.

The way this law can help you is that in case you sell property and hold the financing, you should sell the financing to distance you from the transaction. You might be able to sell it to a related party like a corporation or LLC owned by other family members. But the greater the distance from you the better the protection.

You could also set up a separate financing company, such as an LLC, so it wouldn't even look like you were related. And if the LLC were owned with another family member you would have even more protection.

13 Clean Your Financial Statement

One of the first steps in protecting your assets is to eliminate as many assets as possible from your financial statement. Over the years you have probably added to your assets and proudly watched your wealth grow. When applying for a loan it is only natural to list everything possible and even to exaggerate its value. But for asset protection purposes this is the worst thing you can do.

Your financial statement is one of the first things your creditor will look at when trying to seize your assets. Your creditor's lawyer can force you to provide copies of all financial statements you have prepared in recent years. What if you didn't save copies, or have "lost" them? Creditors can subpoena copies from all banks you have done business with. And how will they find that out? They will subpoena copies of all checks you have written in past years and see who you have been making payments to.

If your financial statement now has things on it such as a boat, a vacation home and a coin collection, you cannot simply stop listing them and pretend they do not exist. You will be asked under oath what happened to them and will be expected to produce receipts or other proof of what you did with them.

There is little you can do today if a lawsuit has already been filed against you. Your best bet is to sell your nonexempt assets and buy exempt assets. (See Chapter 30.) But if you do not have any claims against you now, you can begin today to clean up your financial statement before you are hit with a future claim. If your available assets diminish slowly over the years, you will not look like a "bad guy" who tried to cheat creditors. You merely prudently shifted to other investments.

You don't have to actually rid yourself of your wealth, and you don't have to lie. Your goal is to convert what you have to forms of wealth that either do not appear on your financial statement or are untouchable by your creditors.

There are many ways to convert your assets to safe forms of ownership. The longer the time period before your potential trouble, the more flexibility you have. If you set up an LLC in which you are a 1% (but controlling) member, or a children's trust, you can keep assets such as recreational vehicles and coin collections, but take them off your financial statement.

Immediately before wiping out your debts through bankruptcy you can convert some nonexempt assets to exempt assets (see Chapter 15). But all transfers made within a year of bankruptcy must be disclosed to the court and can be set aside. If you have no financial problems for the next year most transfers you make now will be safe, and if no problems arise for 5 or 10 years, your sales or transfers might not even be questioned.

14 Protect Your Privacy

One important way to protect your assets is to keep your affairs private. People who are obviously wealthy are at a greater risk of being sued. The most famous and wealthy in our society are constantly being sued by people trying to get some of their wealth. For them, defending such suits comes as the cost of being famous.

One of the first things an attorney does when he takes a case is to see what assets the defendant has available. If it looks like a lot of assets are available, the case is well worth taking. Even a frivolous suit might get a settlement to avoid the nuisance and legal fees. But if the defendant appears to have few assets the attorney might try for a quick settlement for a small amount, or accept the limit of the insurance policy, or not take the case at all.

Most personal injury cases in this country are taken on a contingent fee basis by attorneys. This means that the attorneys don't get paid unless the client collects. They may work for nothing for years on a case if it looks like there will be a big payoff in the end. Some of them may even put out thousands of dollars of their own money to pay the costs of investigating and trying the case. But attorneys are not likely to take cases that involve a lot of work and little chance for reward.

To protect your wealth you should keep as low a profile as possible. If you flaunt your wealth, wear expensive jewelry, drive expensive cars and live in a mansion you are more likely to be the target of a lawsuit (and you will have more available assets to seize). Sam Walton, founder of Wal-Mart, was one of the wealthiest men in the world and yet he drove a pickup truck. Does your ego demand more?

You may be thinking, "But what good is it to be wealthy if I cannot enjoy it? I like and want a Porsche, furs, a mansion and my own jet." Okay, if you must have those things you can, but you will face a greater expense in protecting them and a greater risk of lawsuits. The cost to keep them will be much greater than the price to buy them.

Another alternative is to live two life-styles. Where you live and work you can live modestly, but on the weekend you can go to your luxury home in Manhattan, Monte Carlo, or Vail. Tell your neighbors you spend weekends with your mother, or at a cottage in the country.

Another advantage of protecting your privacy is that if you are sued your wealth can less easily be found if you have not left extensive records of it.

In our country today there are hundreds of government and private databases that contain countless facts about your life. Credit bureaus, the social security administration, banks, loan companies, department stores and numerous other entities have files on you. Did you notice how some grocery chains are starting to charge more if you don't sign up for their membership card? (They call it a discount for using the card, but the bottom line is you pay more if you don't.) Just think, somewhere in their computers they can have a list of every food, medicine and toiletry product you bought! Plus they know if you paid cash or used a credit or debit card. What will they do if some day one of your creditors subpoena's their records of your purchases?

Fortunately, some chains will give you a card even if you refuse to give your name and other information. If you use a store which requires a card, ask if you can get one without giving your name. If they require one, see if they check identification. Leave your ID at home and see if they will issue a card. If not, tell them you prefer to shop elsewhere.

Look at your check book and your credit card statements. What do these say about you? Do they list investments? Jewelry purchases? Gifts? Flights overseas? The purchase of this book? All of these records will be available to parties who sue you. In most cases they cannot see them until they win a lawsuit. But in some situations they can subpoena your records early in the case.

If you claim to have "lost" your records they can get copies from your bank. Banks microfilm every check you write, so all of your purchases can all be traced.

The first thing you need to do is to make sure there is no permanent record of your purchases. Don't worry about the basics like your mortgage payment, electricity, water, etc. Everyone has those expenses and it would be silly to drive around town paying cash for those things. But your discretionary purchases should not be made by check or credit card. Or at least not by *your* check or credit card. How do you pay for things? With cash or by check or credit cards which are not in your name.

Legal Issues

Just like a knife, which can either be used to peel an apple or to kill someone, the information in this chapter can be used for honest or dishonest purposes. The purpose of this book is to show you how you can legally protect what you have earned from unfair claimants. It is not a manual on how to avoid taxes or launder money.

One problem with using privacy techniques for asset protection is that it arouses suspicion of the IRS and the United States Department of Justice. If an IRS audit reveals any evidence of cash transactions which were not run through your bank account, you will be suspected of tax fraud. To counter this possible claim you should keep detailed records of your cash transactions which you can produce in the event of an audit.

There are many loopholes and deductions in our tax system. It is not necessary to become a criminal to lower your taxes. Doing so puts an emotional strain on you as well as opens the possibility that you may lose your freedom completely if you are jailed for tax evasion. Don't become a criminal for a few extra dollars. Just use the loopholes in the tax system to pay as little as possible.

As discussed later in this chapter, there are severe penalties for money laundering. In its zest to slow the use of drugs our government has passed several laws which make innocent acts criminal. Be careful not to run afoul of these laws.

Since the tragedy of September 11th, it has become a red flag to do such things as buy an airline ticket with cash. Be careful that your asset protection efforts do not fit you into the terrorist profile.

Cash

The simplest way to avoid having a record of your financial affairs is to use cash. Years ago it was expected that we would soon have a cashless society, but we are now using more cash than ever.

For normal household expenses, checks and credit cards are fine, but for luxury and small investment expenses, cash would be better. Every week when you deposit your paycheck take part of it in cash. Or cash every other paycheck. Here are some other suggestions and things to keep in mind. To prove the cash wasn't untaxed income you should keep a record.

◆ When you receive dividends, bonuses, mortgage payments, or other receivables in the form of checks, you can take them to the bank teller and get cash for them without depositing them into your account. That way they are not microfilmed along with your bank records.

◆ For local checks you can go to the banks on which they are drawn to get cash, but this would not be much of an advantage over cashing them at a bank where you have an account (as long as they are not deposited into the account).

◆ Keep in mind that cashing a check without depositing it does not relieve you of the tax liability, it only gives you privacy as to how you spent it. In many cases you and the IRS will get 1099 statements which report this income.

◆ There is a law which requires all transactions of over $10,000 in cash to be reported to the federal government. If you try to break down a large transaction into several smaller ones over a few days, these are supposed to be combined and reported.

◆ For transactions which must be conducted by mail, money orders or cashier's checks can be used. Some banks even allow a certain number of free cashier's checks a month. However, other banks require that if you buy a money order with cash (even a $5 money order) you must fill out a form with your name, address, social security number, etc. Find a new bank.

◆ If you leave the country with more than $10,000 in cash or negotiable instruments, you are required to file a federal report. There is no limit to the amount you can take out of the country, you just have to report it when you leave. If you are caught leaving with more than $10,000 it can be seized, though one court ruled that the government couldn't keep all of it just for the failure to file a report.

Credit Cards

Since your credit card accounts are reported to the credit bureau, a card in your name and social security number will show up on a copy of your credit report. A creditor's attorney can get a list of your credit cards, and from these a statement of all of your purchases. Therefore, to ensure privacy you need a card which is not listed in your name. These are some possibilities:

◆ If you can get a credit card in a foreign country, it will not be reported to the U.S. credit bureaus. Visa, Master Card and American Express issue cards all over the world which are good in nearly every country. This means that if you get a foreign card you can use it here in the U.S. as a normal card for meals, travel, investments, gifts or anything else.

The problem with this is that it is very hard to get a card elsewhere as a nonresident. Possibly if you open a bank account at the same bank (and authorize payments to be debited from the account) it may help. But in some places you may have to establish a local address. (Any plans for an extended vacation or intensive language study abroad?)

If your foreign account is denominated in a foreign currency you may have to pay a conversion fee for every transaction in the US. To avoid this you may be able to get a foreign account denominated in US dollars.

On Schedule B of IRS form 1040 there is a question of whether you have a foreign financial account. If you read the instructions you will see that you can answer "no" if you did have an account but never had more than $10,000 in the account.

In 2000, a federal court in Miami allowed the IRS to subpoena the records of American Express,

MasterCard and Visa of Americans who had accounts in the Bahamas, the Cayman Islands, and Antigua and Barbuda.

◆ If you have a trusted friend, or rather a friend who trusts you, you can get a credit card in his or her name. For example, ask your parent or child to apply for a credit card and put you on the account as an additional user. Once the card is issued, destroy their card and have the address of the account changed to a post office box to which you have access. Then use the card as your own and pay the bill each month with a money order purchased for cash.

◆ A spouse would not be a good choice because in a divorce all of your records could be disclosed. Also, in a suit against both of you, the records would be available to creditors.

◆ Today banks are eager to issue credit cards to corporations and LLCs. (This is because merchants are charged higher fees to process them.) While the business's records might be subpoenaed, if you held only a minor interest it might be ignored. However, be careful when using a corporate account for personal expenses. If not reimbursed scrupulously, it might result in tax problems or a "piercing of the corporate" veil.

Checking Account

The ideal checking account is one that is not in your name or social security number and does not pay interest (which would result in a 1099 which must go on your tax return). These are some possibilities:

◆ You could set up a corporation or LLC with its own employer identification number (EIN) to get a checking account. You should not use your regular business corporation or LLC because mixing business and personal money is forbidden and record keeping could be a nightmare. But you could set one up just for the account. (If the business makes no income it wouldn't have to pay taxes.)

◆ As with credit cards above, if you have a trusting friend you can open an account in his or her name and social security number and then make all the deposits and checks yourself. (Be sure to be listed as a signatory on the account.)

◆ If you set up a trust you may be able to obtain a separate Federal Employer Identification Number for it. Then you could open a bank account for the trust and use its FEIN instead of your social security number.

◆ While a local bank may be useful for local bills, the bulk of your transactions could be done through a money market account with check writing privileges in another state. This would make it harder for a local creditor to subpoena records or garnish funds.

Whether any or all of these methods work will depend on how clever the attorney is who is after you. It will depend on whether his deposition questions ask for "your personal checking account records," "all checking accounts in your name," or "all checking accounts on which you can sign."

Real Estate

In county courthouses around the country, copies of deeds and the taxes paid on them are public records which allows anyone to look up what was paid for a piece of property. Property appraisers' offices sometimes have data which includes the layout of the house and the value of the fixtures. Today many of these records are available on the Internet, free for everyone in the world to see! There are no public records of the stocks, bonds or bank accounts people own, so why are real estate records open to public view? They don't have to be. There are ways to keep some of this information private.

Land Trusts

One of the best ways to keep real estate ownership secret is the "Illinois-type" land trust. This device allows you to put property in the name of another person, company, or bank, keeping your name off the public records. When the property is transferred, the "deed stamps" can be put on the assignment of the trust certificate, which is not recorded in the public records. No one need know who owns the property, how much it sold for, or even how many times it sold.

Since liability for environmental pollution and lead paint poisoning can extend to all owners of property for the last twenty or more years, a land trust can help by completely shielding your identity. Once a trust is closed the trustee need not keep the records for any set number of years, so there may be no way to find an owner once they have been destroyed.

Land trusts can be used in nearly all states, but in some states it is more difficult to use them than others because they don't have specific laws authorizing them. Arizona, California, Florida, Hawaii, Illinois, Indiana, North Dakota, and Virginia have the best land trust laws or court cases. They can work in other states if the trust is worded correctly. For a summary of each state's land trust laws see the author's book, *Land Trusts for Privacy & Profit*.

Living Trusts

If land trusts are difficult to use in your state you might be able to use a living trust with someone other than yourself, such as a bank, as the trustee. However, since living trusts are often recorded, they are not as good as land trusts for privacy.

Corporations

If a corporation owns a piece of property, stock in the corporation could be sold with no record of the price paid or the purchaser. In most states corporations must disclose their officers and directors, but not the names of their stockholders. If you are buying a piece of property you could arrange for the seller to convey it to a corporation and then transfer the stock to you. However, there are numerous tax considerations involved and such a transaction should be set up by your accountant.

Keep in mind that while the stockholders of a corporation are not registered anywhere, the officers and directors are public record and most are available on the Internet. In many states someone could search the corporate records for all corporations in which you are an officer or director. Therefore it may be advisable to use a relative or friend for these positions.

Using an out of state corporation may make it less easy to find you. Some people promote Nevada as a good state in which to incorporate. But even Nevada lists corporate officers on the Internet.

Limited Liability Companies and Limited Partnerships

Because of the strong asset protection benefits of a limited liability companies and limited partnerships, they are two of the best ways to hold real property. They are discussed in more detail in Chapters 32 and 34.

Aircraft and Boats

If you own an aircraft or boat in your own name it is easy for a creditor to find. It often takes just one phone call. Owning these items through a corporation, LLC or limited partnership can offer both privacy and protection from liability. A trust can also be used for privacy.

Gold and Collectibles

One of the best ways to keep your wealth private is to invest in something of which there is no record. Gold coins, rare stamps, gemstones, and all types of collectibles can be bought for cash at both shops and collectibles shows. Most of these can be easily hidden from thieves. Some collectibles, such as rare toys, porcelain or other antiques can be worth tens of thousands of dollars, yet be ignored by burglars who are unaware of their value.

If you plan to invest in collectibles of this type, be sure it is something you are interested in and willing to learn about. You cannot safely invest in collectibles and expect to rely on the goodwill of dealers. Dealers in collectibles make the most profit from customers who do not know the value of the items. To do well you must enjoy the items enough to become knowledgeable about them. Also, be sure to leave some records for your heirs to find which explain the values and the best ways to get full value for them.

If you own valuable items you will need to protect them from loss. If you insure them there will be a record of the insurance. If you keep them in a safe deposit box there will be a record of the box. Although only you will know what is in the box, if you have a large size box it will be hard to claim you only kept your deed and insurance papers in it.

Some items such as gold and gems can be safely hidden in your home. A secret compartment in a door frame or fake receptacle box will be safe from most burglars. Burying them in the basement under the concrete will probably survive most natural disasters. Just be sure there is a map for your heirs in case you die. You wouldn't want your prize possessions to go to some demolition worker 50 years from now!

Other Ways to Protect Your Privacy

The above are the best things you can do to protect your financial privacy. Some other suggestions are:

- ◆ Use a post office box. If you can conveniently use one in a different town than that of your home that is even better.

- ◆ Do not list your phone number. Or, list your number under a fake name. Then you can tell friends "If you need to look up my number, I'm under 'Bill Ding.'" Today it is possible to buy a CD-ROM containing nearly every phone listing in the country for a few dollars and nearly every phone number can be found on the Internet. (Go to www.google.com and type in your home phone number.)

◆ Use a signature which is unreadable, especially on your checks.

◆ You can use different versions of your real name to confuse persons trying to search your records. For example, Harold Robert Jones could be Harold R. Jones, Harry Jones, H. Robert Jones, H. R. "Bob" Jones or even Bob Jones. This would not be foolproof, since searchers are supposed to check all variations, but it could be missed.

How People Find You

To know how to avoid being found you must know the techniques used to track people down. I have read different books explaining how to find a person and from these learned the following:

◆ The most important piece of information needed to track someone down is their social security number and their date of birth. Therefore, you should never give these out to anyone unless absolutely necessary. Sometimes, people who say that you must give them this information are mistaken. If you are a sole proprietor you have the choice of using your social security number or getting a federal Employer Identification Number. By using the latter you can keep your business separate from your personal affairs.

◆ It is sometimes possible to get a birth date and social security number from a state department of motor vehicles with only a name. But in some states you can refuse to give your social security number. There are presently laws pending to forbid them from requiring it.

- ◆ If you file a change of address form with the post office, anyone can obtain this by paying $1 or by writing "Address correction requested" on a letter sent to you. There are also plans to enter this into a national database. To avoid disclosing your new address this way, you should notify correspondents individually or have your mail forwarded to a post office box. If the box is in a state other than the one you are moving to, you can really throw them off!

- ◆ If you are in any type of regulated profession or hold any type of license, the state records on you are probably open to the public.

- ◆ More and more records are being made available over the Internet. These will include court cases, deed records, recreational permits, tenant records and many others.

Changing Your Name

One thing you may consider if you are serious about not being found is changing your name. Of course, with the same birth date and social security number this is not foolproof, but it may slow down those who do not have this information and are just checking for your name.

In most states you cannot change your name if you have an illegal or ulterior purpose. In your request to change your name you will probably be required to list any judgments against you, any bankruptcies, and other information. Failure to answer truthfully will most likely be considered perjury.

This may not be useful for those who have already had problems, but for those with no pending claims who want to make a fresh start without worrying about events in the past which may come back to haunt them, this may work.

Each state has its own laws for changing names and some may be more useful than others. If the state in which you intend to relocate has laws that will not help you, you may wish to go to another state to change your name. To compare the name change laws of the different states you can check the name change statutes of each state in a large law library. Most law schools have statutes of all the states.

Destroying Records

If you destroy records which are useful in an ongoing legal matter you can be fined or imprisoned for destroying evidence. However, there is no law requiring you to keep records which are not presently needed in court.

To protect your privacy you can regularly destroy your financial records. Of course you need to keep accurate records of your tax records. (Usually for 3 years – check with your accountant.)

If throughout your career you regularly destroyed your records after three years (there just isn't room for all of them) you would not look like a bad guy five or ten or twenty years later when an attorney wants to see your lifetime of records.

If you change bank accounts and credit cards every year or two, then it is not likely you would even remember what accounts you had ten or twenty years earlier. So it would be impossible to subpoena then from the banks.

Criminal Laws

Anyone who wishes to protect his privacy should be aware of the numerous criminal laws regarding money laundering and bank secrecy. Due to their frustration in being unable to catch drug dealers, our government has passed numerous laws making different types of financial secrecy a criminal offense. Also, the events of September 11th have inspired many new attempts to criminalize formerly benign activities.

These laws are very tough and there are few loopholes. Our government does not care that they may catch innocent

Americans. They just want to be sure they can catch the drug dealers. Many innocent Americans have faced criminal penalties and the loss of their savings for honest mistakes. For example, an elderly doctor who kept his savings in cash because he learned to fear banks during the Depression lost his life savings when he made a cash deposit improperly in a friend's bank.

Even local law enforcement agencies are going after Americans who innocently have cash in their possession. Cars travelling on Interstate-95 between Miami and New York which "look suspicious" are being stopped. If cash is found in the car, the cash is seized for no other reason than that it was "suspicious." Sums of $1,000, $3,000 and more are being lost simply because it is too costly to hire a lawyer to retrieve them.

Such formerly innocent acts as paying cash for an airline ticket or travelling without checking luggage are being used to target people for search.

Some of the laws which may affect your efforts to protect your privacy are:

The Bank Secrecy Act of 1970

- Must report cash transactions of over $10,000.

- Must report carrying cash of over $10,000 in or out of the country.

- Must report foreign bank accounts of over $10,000.

- Banks must microfilm all checks over $100 (but most banks copy all checks since it is too much work to sort them).

- Banks must request social security number or Federal Employer Identification Number for all accounts.

The Money Laundering Control Act of 1986

◆ Dealing in the proceeds of certain crimes is illegal and the penalty is up to 20 years in prison and a fine of $500,000 or double the amount involved. One congressman stated that if a grocer knowingly accepts payment for groceries from a drug dealer he may be guilty under this law.

◆ Knowingly attempting to engage in transactions involving $10,000 or more of money from certain criminal sources is illegal and the penalty is up to 10 years in prison and a fine of $250,000 or double the amount involved.

◆ Illegally concealing legitimately-earned money can also be a violation of the act.

◆ Attempting to cause a financial institution to not file a currency transaction report or to file an incorrect one is also a violation.

◆ It is illegal to engage in several smaller transactions to avoid financial reporting requirements. This is called "structuring." Depositing $5,500 in cash into your bank account two days in a row (from the same source) is a felony. The punishment is a mandatory five-year sentence, $250,000 fine, and forfeiture of the funds involved. (A rapist may have to be released to make room for you.)

◆ If you violate any of the last three of these while violating any other law, or in a pattern involving over $100,000 during a one-year period, then the penalty is $500,000 and 10 years in prison.

The Anti-Drug Abuse Act of 1988

◆ Banks must keep logs of money orders, traveler's checks and cashier's checks of more than $3,000.

- ◆ Banks in some areas must keep logs of *all* cash transactions.
- ◆ The Treasury Secretary is authorized to negotiate with foreign countries to start cash reporting systems.

The Annunzio-Wylie Act of 1992

- ◆ Creates a new felony and forfeiture of assets for operating an "illegal money transmitter business" without a state license.

The Money Laundering Suppression Act of 1994

- ◆ Requires registration and reporting by non-bank financial institutions, such as currency exchanges, money transmitters (i.e. Western Union), travelers check issuers, money order sellers, and casinos.
- ◆ Encourages state regulation of these businesses.

The Uniting and Strengthening America by Providing Appropriate Tools to Intercept and Obstruct Terrorism Act of 2001 (USA PATRIOT Act)

- ◆ Requires credit card companies, mutual funds, money order companies and others to implement new anti-money laundering programs.
- ◆ Requires many types of private companies to report suspicious activities.
- ◆ Allows the federal government to review records of libraries and bookstores.

For more information:

For information on what businesses are required to do to watch our transactions, see:

"Money Laundering: A Banker's Guide to Avoiding Problems," at www.occ.treas.gov/launder/orige.htm.

Also, U.S. Department of the Treasury in consultation with the U.S. Department of Justice, "The 2002 National Money Laundering Strategy," at www.ustreas.gov/offices/enforcement/2002.pdf.

Part Three - Protecting Property in Your Name

15 How Exemptions Work

Every state and the federal government provides that certain property is exempt from the claims of creditors. This means that no matter how much you owe, your creditors cannot take certain property from you. In some states the property you can keep is only worth a few thousand dollars, but in other states it can be millions of dollars.

What is exempt is a public policy decision. It is felt that allowing a debtor keep certain property is more important than letting the creditor take everything.

The rationale is that if persons could lose everything they own to creditors, including their home and car and tools of their trade, they would be a burden on society, which would then have to support them. Allowing them to keep some property allows them to get a fresh start.

Most states allow you to keep all your retirement funds. Some allow a home of unlimited size and any funds put into annuities. So the fresh start can be quite a nice one. Former governor John Connolly of Texas used his state's generous bankruptcy laws to shield many of his assets when he got into financial difficulties years after he accompanied President Kennedy through Dallas on that fateful day.

The following chapters discuss the various types of exempt property. Laws vary greatly from state to state so this material is general and discusses the different types of systems. A comparison of the important exemptions is found in some of the chapters, and a summary of the exemptions for each state is in Appendix A. But these laws often change. For a final determination of what is exempt in your state be sure to consult a specialist as discussed in Chapter 49.

There is a set of federal exemptions and a set for each state (except for California which allows two options). Which ones you may use depends upon the state in which you live. In fifteen states and the District of Columbia, debtors have a choice between the state exemptions and the federal exemptions contained in 11 USC §522. The states are: Arkansas, Connecticut, Hawaii, Massachusetts, Michigan, Minnesota, New Hampshire, New Jersey, New Mexico, Pennsylvania, Rhode Island, Texas, Vermont, Washington, Wisconsin. The federal exemptions are as follows. Married couples who file bankruptcy together can double these amounts:

Homestead: $17,425

Vehicle: $2,775

Annuity/Insurance: Yes

Pensions: Yes

Personal Property $9,300+

Tools: $1,750

Business Partnership: No

You can compare these to the ones for your state listed in Appendix A. However, these only give a general idea and you need to look at the exact statutes to learn the details.

In the other states you must use the state exemptions. In these states, and if you choose the state exemptions in any of the above states, you may also use the federal non-bankruptcy exemptions.

Therefore, you should compare the federal exemptions against the exemptions for your state together with the federal non-bankruptcy exemptions.

Converting Nonexempt to Exempt Assets

Since some property is exempt and other property can be taken by creditors, a person with creditors of course would like to get rid of all nonexempt property and own only exempt property. Sometimes this is completely legal, sometimes not. Unfortunately, there are no clear rules as to what is allowed. The important factors in deciding whether your conversion was legal are the state you live in and whether you look to the judge like an honest person or a crook.

It is clear in the Congressional Record that people are allowed to convert their nonexempt assets into exempt assets prior to filing for bankruptcy.

> As under current law, the debtor will be permitted to convert nonexempt property into exempt property before filing a bankruptcy petition. The practice is not fraudulent as to creditors, and permits the debtor to make full use of the exemptions to which he is entitled under the law. H.R.Rep. No. 595, 95th Cong., 1st Sess. 361 (1977); S.Rep. No. 989, 95th Cong., 2nd Sess. 76 (1978).

Some shifting of property can even be done on the "eve of bankruptcy." However, some courts have decided that certain types of shifting do constitute a fraud of creditors. Therefore a person must be careful in his pre-bankruptcy planning not to do anything which may be interpreted as fraud. One thing a court looks at is dealings with creditors. If a person takes actions to deceive his creditors or engages in any clandestine activities, this will look bad to the court.

In a California case, a woman was required as part of her divorce settlement to reimburse her husband for marital debts of nearly $17,000. Two years later when she failed to pay, her husband set a hearing for a writ of execution. She asked for a continuance so that she could get an attorney. It was granted and she then went out and mortgaged the available equity in her house, spent the money and filed bankruptcy. The bankruptcy court admitted that she had the right to convert nonexempt property into exempt property, but found that she had an *intent to defraud* her husband and denied her discharge under § 727(a)(2) of the Bankruptcy Code.

Another court explained that minor actions will be overlooked, but that "when a pig becomes a hog it is slaughtered... wholesale slaughtering of assets which otherwise would go to creditors is not permissible."

Two prohibitions in the bankruptcy laws are that creditors not be "defrauded," (§ 548) and that they not be "hindered or delayed" (§ 727). Clearly converting assets hinders and delays them, but many courts hold that conversion is legal unless the debtor has done something fraudulent (such as lying or hiding assets).

In a recent Florida case a debtor who had a $15 million fraud judgment against him moved from Tennessee to Florida and bought a home for $650,000. Eighteen months later he filed for bankruptcy and the Florida Supreme Court, in advice to the federal courts, ruled that this was legal under Florida homestead law.

But some courts have limited the right to convert assets, saying that this violated the prohibition against hindering and delaying creditors. Keep in mind that there are hundreds of bankruptcy judges throughout the country, not all of them wise and competent, and that on bad days they may make bad decisions.

Since the U. S. Supreme Court has not made a definitive ruling on this subject, the law for your state depends on which federal circuit it is in. A good analysis of the law in each circuit is contained in the following article which can be found in most major law libraries, Norwood, John M., "An Historical Analysis of Pre-Bankruptcy Conversion Cases on a Circuit-By-Circuit Basis," 103 Commercial Law Journal 154 (1998).

As a brief summary, the Fourth (Maryland, North Carolina, South Carolina, Virginia, and West Virginia) and Seventh (Illinois, Indiana, and Wisconsin) Circuits have been the most strict. The Second (New York, Vermont, and Connecticut), Eighth (North and South Dakota, Minnesota, Nebraska, Iowa, Missouri and Arkansas) and Ninth (California, Oregon, Washington, Arizona, Montana, Idaho, Nevada, Alaska, and Hawaii) have allowed the most converting, and other circuits can go either way depending on the case.

One thing which is definitely forbidden is borrowing money with which to buy exempt assets prior to bankruptcy. This is always considered an abuse of the system and a fraud upon the creditor from whom the money was borrowed.

Planning, done years before any claims arise, is the main focus of this book. If this planning is done there will be no worry of any allegations that creditors were defrauded. Buying only exempt assets should become a long-term way of life.

The unfortunate thing about using exemptions is that they do not protect you from all types of claims. Some debts, such as alimony and child support, environmental fines, and other debts which are nondischargeable in bankruptcy may be a claim against your exempt property. For those you need other types of protection which are discussed in part four of this book.

16 State Shopping

Not everyone can pack up and leave their home state. If you have lived your whole life in one town or have long-term business relationships, leaving may be the last thing you want to do. But if you face the possibility of losing everything you own, you should consider at least a temporary relocation.

In some states you can lose nearly everything, while in others you can keep millions of dollars in assets. Isn't it worth a year or two away, to keep from losing your life's earnings? You don't even have to stay full time in a new state. You can take up residency there, but only reside there part of the year.

Fortunately, two of the best states for asset protection are both popular destinations for people leaving their own states: Florida and Texas. In both of these states you can keep a home of unlimited value and also hundreds of thousands of dollars in other assets. Many people who had financial problems elsewhere have moved to these states to protect their fortunes.

For those who don't like warm weather and beaches, the states of Iowa, Kansas, Minnesota, Oklahoma and South Dakota also offer generous exemptions and a wider variety of climate. Surely there is one to suit your tastes.

If you cannot leave your home state at the present, perhaps you can at least buy a vacation home in a safer state. That way you could easily make the move later if a liability crisis arises. It would look much better to move to a home you already own than to purchase one after you get sued.

One thing to keep in mind is that you must be a resident of a state for six months in order to take advantage of that state's exemptions. For the homestead exemption, some states require you to reside in the property you are claiming exempt for that six month period. As discussed elsewhere this may change if Congress ever passes bankruptcy reform.

As will be discussed in Chapter 49, you should consult a specialist in state exemption law before arranging your assets. If you plan to move to another state consult a specialist before you start moving assets to be sure that you understand the laws and that they haven't changed.

17 Equity Stripping

Equity stripping is borrowing money against all of the vulnerable equity you have in your properties and investing it in safe assets which cannot be touched by creditors.

Real estate is a very public asset (unless you use land trusts) and if you own property free and clear you are a great target for a lawsuit. But if the public records show that your properties are all mortgaged to the hilt, you look like a poor target. Even if you sued, a lack of easily seized equity (real estate) can help you settle a suit faster.

Homesteads

In states with small or no homestead exemptions, equity stripping is a great way to protect your home. For example, if you have an expensive home in a state which only allows you a $10,000 homestead exemption, you can mortgage your home so that you only have $10,000 in equity. The money from the mortgage can be used to buy property which is exempt, such as an annuity, or which is hard to reach, such as the interest in an LLC.

Today many banks are offering home equity lines of credit which allow you to take as much of the equity as you need and adjust it quickly.

Investment Property

For non-homestead property, you can do the same thing, but since most loans on investment property cannot exceed 70 to 80% of the equity, you need to be more creative. You cannot make a loan to yourself to hide the equity, but you could finance your properties through a related company such as an LLC owned by other family members, or a trust, or some similar entity.

If the lending company appeared to have no relation to you, your lack of equity could scare off potential lawsuits. Even if it did appear related to you, the realization that the equity was shielded by a limited liability company would help.

In states such as Florida where a mortgage can be owned by a land trust, you can keep the source of the funds completely secret. A company related to the author which can handle financial transactions through a Florida land trust is Federal Funding Group, LLC. See: www.federalfundinggroup.com

18 Future Acquisitions

When doing any financial planning, you must keep in mind any possibilities of future receipts of money or property. For example, if you file bankruptcy and within the next 180 days a relative dies leaving you a large inheritance, your bankruptcy creditors are entitled to that inheritance. Or if someone dies leaving you money while you have an outstanding judgment, creditors may be able to attach your inheritance.

You cannot control the timing of death, but you can suggest that your relatives set up your inheritance to avoid your creditors. For example, a trust can be set up which does not allow you to reach the property for a number of years. Or you can be given an annuity if it is exempt in your jurisdiction.

If you are protecting your assets by putting them in your spouse's name, keep in mind that your spouse may die just before, or during, some financial crisis you face. If this results in all marital assets being in your name, your protection plan may be ruined.

Asset protection for yourself may mean asset protection for relatives. Check with your parents and other relatives. If you expect any inheritances, ask that they be put into an LLC, an irrevocable trust or other device which will protect them from your creditors.

If they hesitate, offer to pay for the legal fees. Explain to them the risks of liability and that you have found ways to protect yourself from ruin. It may save your inheritance from your creditors. They may even be interested in asset protection for themselves.

19 Homestead

Almost all states offer an exemption of a person's homestead from the claims of creditors. Unfortunately, in many states it has a very small dollar limit. For example, in many states it is limited to $5,000 and in Michigan, only $3,500. In a few states it is a lot higher, such as $300,000 in Massachusetts and $125,000 in Nevada. But in most states it is only $5,000 to $25,000.

In Arkansas, D.C., Florida, Iowa, Kansas, Oklahoma, South Dakota and Texas the amount of homestead exemption can be unlimited! This means that you can own a large expensive home in these states and your creditors cannot touch it no matter how big your debts are. Some people have even put gold fixtures in their houses in order to shield their wealth! People who expect financial problems move to these states to protect their wealth.

Of course, the homestead exemption does not protect you from losing your home if you do not pay the mortgage or trust deed on the property itself.

The following text describes the possible protections, requirements and exceptions to protection. But these laws can change and are subject to different judicial interpretations. To be sure of the exact protection in your state you should consult with a specialist as explained in Chapter 49.

What Is Protected

The laws vary greatly from state to state as to what type and amount of homestead is protected. In some states only traditional homes are protected, but in many others condominiums, co-op apartments and mobile homes (with or without land) are protected. Some states limit the physical size of the homestead, and often a homestead outside of a city can be larger than one within city limits.

In some states the dollar limit is based upon the person's interest in the property and in others it is based upon the entire property. For example, suppose a person owned a $100,000 home in a state with a $30,000 exemption, and deeded the property to his children reserving a life estate for himself. In a state which only counted the value of the interest, the life estate might be safe from creditors if its value was determined to be less than $30,000. However, in a state which values the entire property, the creditors could reach part of the value.

If the value of the homestead is greater than the exemption, then the homestead can be sold with the amount of the exemption paid to the owner and the balance to the creditor. In some cases, if the homestead is divisible, such as a farm, part of it can be sold off to reduce the homestead to the amount allowed by law.

In most states, upon the death of the owner, the homestead passes to the spouse and/or children free of the claims of the decedent's creditors.

If the homestead burns down, the insurance money to replace the dwelling usually is exempt from creditors' claims also. In some states the homestead may be sold and the proceeds are exempt from creditors' claims for a reasonable length of time so that the person can purchase another homestead.

In many cases homestead rights have been liberally construed and people have been allowed to keep oil and gas rights, crops growing on the property and expensive additions to the property.

In Florida, one of the few states with an unlimited homestead exemption, a married couple which lived separately in two different homes was able to have both homes exempt from creditors. *In re Colwell*, 196 F.3d 1225 (11th Cir. 1999).

Requirements to Protect Homestead

In most states a person does not need to make any special declaration to obtain homestead protection. However, in some states this is necessary; if there is any doubt then a declaration of homestead should be filed in the appropriate records. This is especially true if a judgment is imminent. If a declaration is required you must be sure to strictly comply with the exact requirements of the law. Any error could cause loss of the homestead exemption.

In some states the protection of a homestead applies to any person, but in others only the head of a household is entitled to protection. This means that the person must support a spouse or child.

In most states a person must actually occupy the homestead for protection to apply. However, there are some exceptions if there is evidence that the person has a bona fide intent to make the property his or her homestead.

Usually, though, you must be domiciled in the homestead most of the time during the 180 days preceding your filing for bankruptcy to insure the exemption. Different bankruptcy reform proposals before Congress require ownership or living in the homestead for up to four years. If any of these proposals pass, you should find out exactly what the rules are.

Exceptions to Homestead Protection

There are various exceptions to the protection afforded by homestead laws and they, of course, also vary by state. The following are some of the exceptions which apply in some of the states. If you have any of these types of debts you should check your state's rules before you attempt to use the homestead exemption to protect equity.

- ◆ debts incurred before the homestead is purchased
- ◆ debts incurred in purchasing the homestead
- ◆ debts incurred before establishment of the homestead
- ◆ debts incurred in improving the homestead
- ◆ debts owed for taxes
- ◆ debts owed for torts committed by the owner
- ◆ debts for alimony
- ◆ criminal penalties
- ◆ claims of parties who have a prior interest in the homestead
- ◆ judgments filed before the homestead is purchased

Note that in some states, such as Maine, the homestead is not protected against tort claims. These would include claims for malpractice and accidents. In these states the homestead is not of much value for asset protection.

In at least one case a person who filed a Chapter 11 bankruptcy (to reorganize debts) and then switched to a Chapter 7 (to discharge debts), a lien which attached to the homestead in the Chapter 11 case could not be discharged.

Not all of these exceptions apply in all states. If you have any of these types of debts and they are exceptions to homestead in your state, you would be wise to pay those debts before paying other debts (provided, of course, that you do not violate any bankruptcy rules against preferring one creditor over another; see Chapter 44).

Loss of Homestead Status

The protection of the homestead can be lost in some states if certain requirements are not complied with. For example, if the owner abandons the property or begins using it for a business instead of a home, the protection may be lost. However, some states allow the homestead to be used for a business as well as a residence. In states which only grant homestead status to the head of a household, the status may be lost if the parties divorce or if child custody changes.

Going into a nursing home, or temporarily moving in with relatives due to an illness, should not cause loss of homestead as long as the person has the intent to return to the homestead eventually.

Homestead Planning

Whatever state you live in, you should carefully plan the equity in your home to protect it from creditors.

If you live in a state with a low homestead exemption you should keep very little equity in your home. If you have a small mortgage or you own your home free and clear, you should refinance it and put the money in an investment that is free from the claims of creditors. You can also get an equity line against your home which allows you to withdraw equity at any time. However, you are limited in what you can do once a claim has been made or if you are contemplating bankruptcy. See Chapter 30 about shifting assets.

If you live in a state with a large homestead exemption you can protect your estate from creditors by having most or all of your net worth in your home. However, you must also consider the chance of divorce as a risk against your assets.

For a couple with joint funds in a state with a large homestead exemption, it is a good idea to pay off the home as quickly as possible. For an individual with the risk of marital problems in the future, other exempt property and offshore (foreign) trusts are better.

Tenancy by the Entireties

In states with low or no homestead exemption, the law of tenancy by the entireties property may protect the homestead from creditors. See the chart on the next page and the next chapter.

Creative Planning

There are some very creative ways to protect the homestead in states with low exemptions. For example, the homestead can be split into different interests and only a portion up to the homestead exemption can be left in the name of the person wishing to be protected. This can be done with life estates or a split interest trust. In a GRIT, a Grantor Retained Interest Trust, the grantor can keep the right to live in the property, and other interests can be owned by the spouse, children or other family members.

Another possibility where the exemption is low is to put the homestead into a partnership, since partnership property cannot be partitioned.

All of these methods require expertise in the field of estate planning, and should not be attempted without consulting an expert.

Your State's Exemption

The homestead limits for each state are listed on the next page. However, for the special rules and limitations you should check with a local attorney who specializes in bankruptcy law to see exactly what is protected in your area.

State Homestead Exemptions

Alabama	$5000	Montana	$60,000
Alaska	$64,800	Nebraska	$12,500
Arizona	$100,000	Nevada	$125,000
Arkansas	Unlimited	New Hamp.	$30,000
California – A	$50,000	New Jersey	None
California – B	$17,425	New Mexico	$30,000
Connecticut	$75,000	New York	$10,000
Delaware	None	North Carolina	$10,000
D. of C.	Any	North Dakota	$80,000
Florida	Unlimited	Ohio	$5,000
Georgia	$10,000	Oklahoma	Unlimited
Hawaii	$20,000	Oregon	$25,000
Idaho	$50,000	Pennsylvania	None
Illinois	$7,500	Rhode Island	$150,000
Indiana	$7,500	South Carolina	$5,000
Iowa	Unlimited	South Dakota	Unlimited
Kansas	Unlimited	Tennessee	$5,000
Kentucky	$5,000	Texas	Unlimited
Louisiana	$25,000	Utah	$20,000
Maine	$25,000	Vermont	$75,000
Maryland	None	Virginia	$5,000
Massachusetts	$300,000	Washington	$40,000
Michigan	$3,500	West Virginia	$25,000
Minnesota	$200,000	Wisconsin	$40,000
Mississippi	$75,000	Wyoming	$10,000
Missouri	$8,000		

20 Tenancy by the Entireties

Joint Tenancy

Contrary to the belief of some, property merely in joint names is not safe from creditors. In most states joint property may be seized by creditors at least to the extent of the debtor's interest. If both parties are on the debt the entire property can be seized.

Joint tenancy with right of survivorship is ownership of property where the survivor owns the entire property upon the death of the other owner. **Tenancy in common** is ownership in which the death of one owner results in that person's interest going to his or her heirs.

In the rare instance where a creditor makes a claim and a debtor dies before the creditor seizes his joint property, the property would pass safely to the other owner. However, in most cases joint ownership of property is not a safe way to own property. In fact it could be more risky than individual ownership because it is subject to both parties' debts.

Some people put their property into joint ownership with their children to avoid probate. This works fine in avoiding probate, but it puts the property at risk of the children's creditors. If your children are involved in an accident or divorce after you put property jointly into their names you may lose part of it.

Community Property

In states which have adopted the community property system (Arizona, California, Idaho, Louisiana, Nevada, New Mexico, Texas, Washington and Wisconsin), there is a special problem with asset protection. Under community property principles, each spouse is considered to own an interest in community property, which is all property acquired during the marriage (other than gifts and inheritances). It does not matter in whose name the property is titled, all property acquired by either party during marriage automatically becomes community property, belonging to both.

Because both spouses have an interest in all community property, certain creditors of either spouse can make claims against all such property. As an example, all personal property bought by a wife with her own earnings can be seized by someone who has a claim against her husband. In addition, when one spouse in a community property state files for bankruptcy, all community property comes under the control of the bankruptcy trustee.

To avoid this problem, the parties can enter into a marital agreement stating that they agree to abandon the community property system and hold their property separately. While a spouse with few assets would probably object to signing such an agreement with a highly successful spouse, the risks to their own assets should make it worthwhile. To make the arrangement more desirable, regular gifts can be made by the wealthy spouse to equalize the assets.

A marital agreement is a complicated document and must comply with state laws in order to be valid. To be sure you have one which is legally enforceable, you should consult a specialist in family law.

Tenancy by the Entireties

In about half of the states the concept of "tenancy by the entireties" is recognized. Under this arrangement property owned by a married couple is considered to be owned by the couple as a unit and not as individuals. Neither party individually has the right to sell the property or any interest in it. Consequently, in some of the states that recognize this concept creditors of one spouse cannot reach property owned in a tenancy by the entireties.

Thus tenancy by the entireties can be a good way to protect the homestead in states that do not give a large exemption to the homestead. Of course, you will have to be careful to avoid liabilities that attach to both spouses if you plan to use tenancy by the entireties protection.

States that recognize tenancy by the entireties property always allow it for real estate but in some states it can also include personal property. Therefore, in those states which protect it from creditors, it can be used to shield numerous items of personal property from creditors.

The first problem people have in protecting their tenancy by the entireties property from creditors is convincing a court that the property is actually held in a tenancy by the entireties. In some states joint ownership by spouses is assumed to be ownership by the entireties but in others it is assumed not to be unless it is clearly spelled out in the purchase or title to the property.

The classic legal requirement for a tenancy by the entirety is that it must be created with five "unities": unity of possession (each party is entitled to possess the property), unity of interest (each party has an equal interest in the property), unity of title (each party must have acquired ownership from the same conveyance), unity of time (the interest of each party must have been created at the same time), and unity of person (the parties must be married which makes them legally one person). In some states a spouse can create tenancy by the entireties property by signing a paper giving his property to himself and his spouse, but in other states it can only be done by having property come from another person.

The only way to be sure your property is protected (if you live in a state which has tenancy by the entireties) is to execute documents which legally create a tenancy by the entirety in the property you want protected. The safest way to do this is by conveying the property first to another person (a "strawman") who conveys it back to you and your spouse in an estate by the entireties. The forms for doing this are included in this book. The strawman can be your parent, sibling or child, but be sure that the person you choose is over 18 years of age and does not have any judgments against him or her.

Any property which was acquired before marriage, even if it was acquired in the names of both spouses, must be retitled in the parties names after marriage. The reason for this is that before marriage it is impossible to own property in a tenancy by the entireties, and it does not change into entireties ownership at marriage. So it must be reconveyed after marriage.

When buying a new piece of property you can be sure that it is held in a tenancy by the entireties by having it so stated on the bill of sale or invoice. If you plan to use the protection of tenancy by the entireties you should have the salesperson put language similar to the following on the paperwork whenever you buy furniture, appliances, electronics or similar items:

```
John Smith and Mary Smith, husband and
wife in a tenancy by the entireties
```

The second possible problem arises when a person converts other property into entireties property within a year prior to filing bankruptcy. Transfers during this time period are often considered frauds against creditors. For this reason it is important to properly set up your property as soon as possible, or to delay bankruptcy for the necessary year.

It should be noted that entireties property is only protected against claims against one spouse. If there are any debts which are joint, those creditors can seize the property and it can be brought into bankruptcy. For this reason spouses should avoid co-signing on each others' debts whenever possible.

Of course, putting property into tenancy by the entireties will not protect it from claims by your spouse. In fact it may make it easier for your spouse to take it. A doctor in San Antonio put numerous assets in the name of his wife to protect them from creditors' claims and the next week she filed for divorce. If avoiding potential spousal claims is of concern to you, you should avoid this arrangement and use a limited liability company or family limited partnership. In states which do not recognize tenancies by the entireties, it may be possible to obtain similar protection through husband and wife A-B living trusts.

In some states the placing of property in the name of both spouses is assumed by law to be a gift unless there is written evidence to the contrary. To avoid this you should put a statement on any deeds or other transfer papers that the spouse's name is being added "for estate planning purposes only and not as a present gift."

One possible problem with entireties property is that if one party files bankruptcy and there is a loan on the property, the trustee may bring the property into the bankruptcy. Therefore it is important that no loans in the debtor's name are on the property at the time of bankruptcy. Also, if the entire interest in the property is acquired by the debtor within 6 months of bankruptcy, the bankruptcy case may be reopened.

Unfortunately, the laws regarding tenancy by the entireties property are not clearly-written statutes, they are mostly court cases which sometimes conflict with statutes. Several sources the author checked all disagree as to which states recognize tenancy by the entireties, and what it protects.

On the following page is a table of the best information available for each state. See the footnotes at the bottom for the protections available. A court case is cited if available, so that you or your attorney may do some research to be sure of your state's current position. For a thorough explanation of tenancy by the entireties law see §52 in *Powell on Real Property* (a multi-volume set of law books available in most law libraries).

A recent article on the status of tenancy by the entireties property in bankruptcy by Illinois Bankruptcy Judge Eugene R. Wedoff is available here:

http://www.ilnb.uscourts.gov/JudgeWedoff/Opinions/TBEoutline.pdf

Complete Guide to Asset Protection Strategies

Tenancy by the Entireties Property Laws

State	Status	Citation
Alabama	Conflicting law	
Alaska	Yes ‡	Alaska Stat § 34.15.140(a) *Pilip v. U.S.* 186 F.Supp.397 (D. Ak 1960)
Arizona	Conflicting law	
Arkansas	Yes ‡	*Morris v. Solesbee*, 892 SW2d 281 (1995)
California	No	
Colorado	Conflicting law	*Tenancy by the Entirety in Colorado*, 13 Colo. Law 230 (1984)
Connecticut	No	
Delaware	Yes*∆	*Citizens Sav. Bank v. Astrin*, 44 Del. 451, 61 A.2d419 (1948)
Dist. of Col.	Yes*∆	*Est. of Wall*, 440 F.2d 215 (D.C.Cir. 1971)
Florida	Yes*∆	*Hunt v. Covington*, 145 Fla. 406, 200 So. 76 (1941)
Georgia	Unclear	*State v. Jackson*, 399 SE2d 88 (1990)
Hawaii	Yes*∆	*In re Cataldo*, 224 BR 426 (9th Cir. BAP 1998)
Idaho	Unclear	
Illinois	Yes	*Travelers v. Engel*, 81 F3d 711 (7th Cir. 1996)
Indiana	Yes∆	*Myler v. Myler*, 137 Ind. App. 605, 210 N.E.2d 446 (1965)
Iowa	Unclear	
Kansas	Conflicting law	
Kentucky	Yes‡	Ky. Rev. Stat. 381.050, -.120, -.135; 389A.030
Louisiana	No	
Maine	No	
Maryland	Yes*∆	*Watterson v. Edgerly*, 40 Md. App. 230, 388 A.2d 934 (1978)
Mass.	Yes*	MGLA §209-1
Michigan	Yes∆	*Cole v. Cardoza*, 441 F.2d 1337 (6 Cir. 1971)
Minnesota	No	
Mississippi	Yes	*Ayers v. Petro*, 417 So2d 912 (Miss 1982)
Missouri	Yes*∆	*Hanebrink v. Tower*, 321 S.W.2d 524 (Mo.Ct.App. 1959)
Montana	No	
Nebraska	Yes	Neb. Rev. Stat. §§ 30-2354, -2637; 36-702; 67-307, -410
Nevada	No	
New Hamp.	No	
New Jersey	Yes°	*Freda v. Comm. Tr. Ins. Co.*, 570 A2d 409 (NJ 1990)
New Mexico	No	
New York	Yes‡	*Berlin v. Herbert*, 265 NYS2d 25 (1965)
N. Carolina	Yes∆	*Hodge v. Hodge*, 12 N.C.App. 574, 183 S.E.2d 800 (1971)
N. Dakota	No	
Ohio	Unclear	*In re Pernus*, 143 BR 856 (N.D.Ohio 1992)
Oklahoma	Yes*	Ok. Stat. tit. 60, § 74
Oregon	Yes*‡	*Brownley v. Lincoln Co.*, 218 Or. 7, 343 P.2d 529 (1959)
Pennsylvania	Yes*∆	*In re Barsotti*, 7 BR 205 (Bkr. W.D.Pa. 1980)
Rhode Island	Yes*∆	*Bloomfield v. Brown*, 67 R.I. 452, 25 A.2d 354 (1942)
S. Carolina	Conflicting law	
S. Dakota	No	
Tennessee	Yes*‡	*C & S Nat'l. Bank v. Aver*, 640 F.2d 837 (6 Cir. 1981)
Texas	Unclear	
Utah	Unclear	
Vermont	Yes*∆	*Lowell v. Lowell*, 138 Vt. 514, 419 A.2d 321 (1980)
Virginia	Yes*∆	*In re Bishop*, 482 F.2d 381 (4 Cir. 1973)
Washington	No	
W.Virginia	No	
Wisconsin	No	
Wyoming	Yes*∆	*Ward Terry v. Hensen*, 75 Wyo. 444, 297 P.2d 213 (1956)

* In these states T/E appears to apply to personal property as well as real estate.
∆ In these states T/E property is strongly protected from creditors.
‡ In these states creditors have some rights to T/E property.
° In NJ Creditors can reach T/E property.

21 Pensions & Retirement Accounts

A pension plan can be one of the best parts of an asset protection plan. Because the public policy is to not allow people to enter old age destitute, properly set up retirement plans are exempt from creditors' claims. In one case even a convicted embezzler was allowed to keep his pension plan.

However, pension plans do not provide protection against all types of creditors. They are not safe from such things as spouse or child support obligations and environmental fines. If you expect liabilities of these types you should avoid using pension plans for protection. If you are not yet married and expect to be able to use a premarital agreement to protect yourself from alimony, be sure to protect your pension in the agreement. In negotiating a premarital agreement, asking for a waiver of claims against a pension plan should be one of the easiest points. "You wouldn't ever take my pension plan would you???" (Use that sad puppy dog look!)

ERISA Plans

Prior to 1992 there was a split between the different courts in this country as to whether ERISA plans were exempt in bankruptcy. (ERISA plans are those covered by the federal Employee Retirement Income Security Act.) But in an important case the United States Supreme Court held that they were excluded from the bankruptcy estate under 11 U.S.C. §541(c)(2). ERISA plans are also exempt from creditors' claims outside of bankruptcy. This means that they cannot be seized or garnished.

ERISA plans include pension plans (defined benefit plans), voluntary plans (401(k) plans), and profit sharing plans (defined contribution plans). However, not all plans are ERISA-qualified so you should consult the director of your plan or an attorney who specializes in ERISA law to see if your plan is qualified.

One exception to the protection for ERISA plans is if it only benefits the owner of a business. Such plans do not qualify. To solve this problem you might be able to add an employee to the plan to make it qualify. A dentist in New York had nearly $400,000 in his Keogh plan when he filed bankruptcy, expecting to keep it all. But because he did not make the minimum contributions for his employees, the money in his plan went to his creditors. In another case a man had $430,000 in his plan but lost it because he didn't follow the terms, and used it as his "personal piggy bank" taking loans from it.

If you have a plan in your own company you should be sure to have it by an expert to see if it complies with the law. Pension plan laws are among the most complex devised by man. Specific documentation is required, actuarial figures must be calculated correctly, and status reports must be timely filed. Mistakes could disqualify your plan for both asset protection and favorable tax treatment.

IRAs and Non-Qualified Plans

IRAs and non-qualified plans do not contain the important language which makes them non-transferable, so they must be turned over to the bankruptcy trustee unless your state has a specific provision making them exempt. Most states exempt pensions for public employees such as teachers and police, but some exempt all IRAs. In some states you can roll over a non-exempt IRA into an exempt pension plan.

In some states only amounts "needed for support" are exempt, but in others all IRA money is exempt, no matter how much there is. What is needed for support usually depends upon the age of the debtor. A 65-year-old might need his entire pension plan, whereas a 45-year-old could be considered young enough to start saving anew and could lose his entire account.

States that have laws that exempt many pension plans include California, Georgia, Idaho, Indiana, Iowa, Pennsylvania, Texas and Washington. States that exempt IRAs include California, Florida, Massachusetts and Texas.

The limits on contributions to IRS and other pension plans are being raised gradually. The following are the limits for traditional and Roth IRAs from 2003 through 2009. Those aged 50 and higher can put in an additional $500 in 2003 to 2005 and an additional $1000 in 2006 to 2009.

2003-4	$3,000
2005-7	$4,000
2008-9	$5,000

Simple IRAs allow contributions of $8,000 to $10,000 in 2003 through 2005 and then they are indexed. For SEP IRAs the maximum is 25% of your salary up to $40,000 a year.

Roth IRAs

The original IRA was a system where you could put money into a retirement account, take it as a tax deduction, and have the earning build up tax-free. You would only pay tax when you took money out of the account. The Roth IRA is a newer plan in which your contributions are not tax deductible, the earnings are not taxable, and what you take out is not taxable.

If your only earnings are a pitiful 1% or 2% a year of interest, then probably the Roth IRA is not as beneficial to you as a traditional IRA where you can deduct the whole contribution. But the Roth IRA works best when you can get a great return on an investment and it is all tax free.

For example, suppose you had just $10,000 in your Roth IRA and bought an option on a property you knew was going to go up in value. In a few years you might be able to exercise the option and get a $50,000 profit for your Roth IRA. The entire amount would be tax-free.

There are many ways to use a Roth IRA to convert taxable income to tax-free income, but such a discussion is beyond the scope of this book. The important things you should know are:

- ◆ The most profitable ways to use a Roth IRA must be done through a self-directed account. Most banks and mutual fund companies don't provide these accounts, or if they do, do not allow creative investments such as real estate and options.

- ◆ You must avoid self-dealing. You can't buy an option on property you own or buy from or sell to your own IRA. You can't even use family members. Some people use a circle of friends, but you still need to be careful not to set up a deal where you each help each other. Three-way or four-way deals are best.

Divorce

There are rules for pension plans that can have unexpected results in divorce. Because of spousal rights a spouse cannot be eliminated as beneficiary without a signed consent. For example, one man changed his beneficiary to his brother during divorce, but when he died after the divorce the assets still went to his ex-wife. Why? Because the change was ineffective while he was married. He should have waited until after the divorce to make the change.

22 Wages

Every state has an exemption for some types of income. These may include wages, salary, social security, welfare, or unemployment compensation. Some exemptions apply only to heads of households (you must have at least one person who is dependent on you) but many apply to anyone. In some states earnings of independent contractors or sole owners of corporations are not considered exempt wages.

In addition to the state laws, there is a federal exemption for certain wages. In most states at least a portion of unpaid wages are exempt, and in some states, such as Florida, even wages which have been received and placed in a bank account are exempt.

In a state with this rule, even if you have several thousand dollars in the bank, if the source of the money was your wages, you creditors cannot touch it. However, states which exempt wages often have rules that, to be exempt, the wages must not be commingled with other funds. If you have any other income in the account, such as a spouse's income, or even interest earned on the account, the court could take away the exemption for the entire account. In one case, because a person's paycheck included reimbursement for expenses, the exemption was denied.

If wages are exempt in your state you should put them in a separate account and not deposit any other funds in that account. You cannot even let interest on the wages be mixed with them. If the account pays interest, see if it can be credited to another account or issued as a check each month or each quarter. If you have other sources of income, such as rents, royalties, dividends or interest, you should live on that money and let your wages accumulate.

The same situation applies to social security payments. If they are deposited in a separate account they can be exempt from creditors' claims. The rationale for the exemption is that such funds provide needed support, but creditors have argued that if a person has other support social security funds should not be exempt. However, the U. S. Supreme Court held that these funds are exempt even if a person has other support.

There are cases, though, which hold that the exemption is not absolute. In one case in which a person commingled social security funds with other money and fled to Switzerland with millions of dollars, the court held the funds not exempt. The lesson is to keep the funds in a separate account (and to spend nonexempt funds).

Courts have held that income which is received by independent contractors is not exempt because it is not technically wages. If you are an independent contractor, you may be able to get around this problem by incorporating your business and hiring yourself as an employee. In some states your salary from the corporation would then be considered wages. Incorporation could also offer other benefits.

The Consumer Credit Protection Act (15 U.S.C. §§ 1601-1692r) also provides an exemption for wages.

23 Life Insurance

Life insurance can be used for asset protection as well as estate planning. Both federal law and the laws of each state include some exemptions for the cash value or the proceeds of life insurance. Like other exemptions, the amount protected from creditors varies from state to state.

There are two basic types of life insurance, term life, in which you pay only for a death benefit, and whole life, in which you pay additional money which builds up as savings. Exemptions in most states protect at least some of this value from creditors' claims. Upon your death, in most states, the proceeds can pass to your beneficiaries free of any claims of your creditors.

The bankruptcy code exempts life insurance in §522(d)(7) and (8). Subsection 7 exempts any unmatured policy and subsection 8 exempts any policy with a cash value of less than $4,000. States have their own laws regarding what is exempt and some have limits while others do not.

In some states property which is purchased with the proceeds of a life insurance policy are exempt.

In tax planning, life insurance offers a way either to avoid estate taxes or to provide the funds to pay them. For persons whose estates are large but who have little cash, life insurance can make sure that state property will not have to be sold at death. And as discussed later in this chapter, giving away the ownership of a policy takes it out of your estate for tax purposes.

Exceptions to Protections

In some states a life insurance policy is exempt from creditors' claims only if the beneficiaries are the spouse, children or other dependent. In some states the owner of the policy can have the power to change the beneficiary, but in others such a policy would not be protected.

Even if a policy is originally exempt, there are ways that the protections can be lost. One simple way is if you assign your policy to a creditor. While you might not think you would do such a thing, often loan papers prepared by banks contain clauses which can give them a right to your policies. *Never sign loan documents without reading them carefully or having your attorney review them!*

If you buy a policy, pay the premium on a policy at a time when you are insolvent, or use funds which would constitute a fraudulent conveyance, your life insurance policy could be challenged and found to be nonexempt. Changing the beneficiary while insolvent could also cause loss of protection.

Insurance Owned By Another

In states where only a small amount of insurance protected, it is still possible to protect your policy from creditors.

If an insurance policy against your life is owned by another person it cannot be reached by your creditors because it is not your property. It is also excluded from your estate at death for tax purposes.

If you presently have a life insurance policy, you could make a gift of it to your spouse or children. Or if you plan to purchase one in the future you could set it up with them as the owners. However, the transaction should be set up carefully to avoid liability for a gift tax. Since a person is allowed to make gifts of $11,000 per person per year tax free, it is best to structure the transaction to make a gift of $11,000 in value each year.

In order for this protection to work the gift must be absolute. If you retain any control over the policy you may lose both the asset protection and the tax benefits. Also, if you die within three years of transfer of the policy, the amount of insurance may be included in your estate. It is sometimes possible to get around this by using corporations or trusts to supply the funds to the person to purchase the insurance.

Irrevocable Life Insurance Trust

Using an irrevocable life insurance trust can provide both extra asset protection and tax savings. This is because a policy in a trust is not part of a person's assets or estate at death. However, setting up the trust may constitute a taxable gift.

To use such a trust, a person transfers to an irrevocable trust either an existing policy or the funds with which to buy a policy. If additional premiums must be paid, the funds for these can be also paid to the trust. By giving the beneficiaries certain powers to make withdrawals, the payments can qualify for the annual gift tax exclusion of $11,000 per year.

The three-year rule mentioned above also applies to policies transferred to trusts. Again, if the trust purchases the policy with its own funds the three-year rule may not apply.

In community property states there is another complication. If the insurance is purchased with community funds, the surviving spouse may be considered a half owner of the policy. This can be avoided if the policy is purchased with separate funds of the insured spouse.

24 Annuities

In states which protect them from creditors, annuities can seem too good to be true. They offer the flexibility of a mutual fund with the tax advantages of an unlimited IRA, and your creditors can never touch them! Even in states which allow creditors to reach annuities, setting them up outside the country may provide the needed protection.

An annuity is an agreement whereby a person is to get a sum of money regularly over a period of years. There are fixed annuities where the amounts are determined in the beginning, and variable annuities where the amount to be paid out depends upon the return on investment.

Annuities can be set up in several ways. You can pay a lump sum to a company for regular payments which will begin either immediately or at a date in the future. Or you can make periodic payments for a number of years, at which time payments will begin to come to you.

Annuities are useful in asset protection planning because they are exempt from claims in several states. The exemption ranges from $350 (in Arkansas) to an unlimited amount (in Florida). In some states all annuities are exempt, while in others only annuities payable to the spouse, children or other dependents of the debtor are exempt. Under bankruptcy law in every state annuities are exempt up to the amount "needed for support" of the debtor and his or her spouse and dependents.

In different states and in different courts of a state, annuities are given different protection. In one state a bankruptcy court held that lottery winnings would be exempt because they were structured as an annuity. At about the same time another bankruptcy court in the same state held that lottery winnings were not exempt because the annuity was set up to benefit the state paying the winnings, not to benefit the winner.

In some states annuities are only protected if they are "unmatured." That is, if the payments to the debtor have not yet started. In other states this factor does not matter.

In some states such as Florida, annuities have especially strong protection. In one case a woman who was injured in an auto accident had her million dollar settlement structured as an annuity. Years later when she caused an accident herself, her victim was not able to get anything from her. The Florida Supreme Court said that this was an unfair result but that they didn't want to change the law. (Though they had no qualms about trying to change the presidential election!)

In recent years large mutual fund companies such as Fidelity, Vanguard, Dreyfus and Scudder have begun to offer variable annuities. These investments are similar to their other mutual funds, and offer an array of investment choices, but charge slightly higher fees to cover the insurance component. (You are guaranteed that your heirs will get at least what you invested if you die before your payments begin.) Today there are dozens of varieties to choose from and if you choose one in a family of funds then you can switch investments whenever the economy warrants it.

One of the best benefits currently available with annuities is the tax-free compounding of the investment, since the interest is not taxable until it is paid out. In effect it is like an IRA with no limit to the amount you can contribute!

Articles in the press about annuities point out that the returns are a bit lower than a regular mutual fund, and claim that you must be in a high tax bracket to benefit. However, they rarely mention that annuities can be safe from creditors' claims. This benefit more than makes up for the slightly lower return.

Offshore Annuities

An especially useful annuity is one issued by insurance companies in Switzerland. Besides the protection some states offer for annuities, Swiss law provides that if the beneficiary is one's spouse or children, or if the beneficiary is made irrevocable, the annuity cannot be reached by creditors. Even if a U.S. court ordered you to cash it in, Swiss law would protect it.

Some Swiss companies offer the choice of having your investment in U.S. dollars, Swiss francs, British pounds, or euros. For a small fee you can switch currencies at any time.

An added benefit of a foreign annuity is that if it is set up properly it is not considered a foreign bank account, it is considered an insurance policy. Therefore, you do not have to report your annuity on your income tax return in the place where you are asked if you have any foreign bank accounts.

As for safety, the Swiss franc is backed by gold at a mere fraction of its market value and the Swiss insurance companies are among the most solvent in the world, with reserves far higher than the best U.S. companies.

Private Annuities

It is possible to set up an annuity with a private party, such as a relative. One woman transferred property to her daughter as trustee in exchange for an annuity. Later she filed bankruptcy. Because there was no fraudulent intent at the time she set up the arrangement, it was held by the bankruptcy court to be free from her creditor's claims.

A transfer of property in exchange for an annuity of the same value would not normally be considered a fraudulent transfer because it is an equal exchange. In most cases it would be a legal conversion of nonexempt property for exempt property. Of course you must have trust in the person to whom you transfer your property.

Protecting Receivables

Besides purchasing an annuity as an investment, annuities can be used to structure receivables. If you expect to receive an inheritance, court settlement, or other large sum of money in the future, you can ask that it be set up as an annuity rather than a straight cash payment.

At least one court held that state lottery winnings spread over several years are not a protected annuity. Therefore, if you win the lottery, you should take a lump sum and invest it in a genuine annuity.

Resources:

Vanguard offers some of the lowest fees on variable annuities 800-522-5555.   http://www.vanguard.com/

Other highly-rated annuities are offered by:

    Fidelity Management & Research, 800-544-2442
        http://www.fidelity.com/

    Scudder Horizon, 800-621-1048
        http://www.scudder.com

Two sources for Swiss annuities are:

JML Jürg M. Lattmann AG
Baarerstrasse 53
CH-6304 Zug
Switzerland
Tel. 011-41-42-265500
Fax: 011-41-42-265590

B.F.I. Consulting AG
Lohwisstrasse 48
CH-8123 Ebmatingen
Switzerland
Tel. 011-41-1-9804254
Fax: 011-41-1-9804255

A good source of more detailed information on offshore annuities is the Offshore Press web site

http://www.offshorepress.com/osva-info.htm

25 Tools of Trade

Most states exempt some "tools of trade" from the claims of creditors. In some states only military uniforms are exempt but in others thousands of dollars in business equipment and books are free from claims. The following is a list of states and the value of the tools of trade which are exempt. In some states there are special rules for certain occupations such as farming. Some states offer no specific exemption for tools of trade, but such items could be exempt from creditors' claims if they are included in the general personal property exemption.

If you need more equipment in your business than your state's exemption allows, you should lease it and limit your equity to the amount allowed as exempt. One possibility is to set up a trust for your children (see Chapter 36) which can purchase the property and lease it to your business. This also allows you to shift income to the children for education or other purposes.

Exemptions for "Tools of Trade"

	Amount	Special rules for:
Federal	$1,750	
Alabama	None	Military personnel
Alaska	$3,360	
Arizona	$2,500	Military personnel, teachers
Arkansas	$750	
California sys. 1	$5,000	Spouse, vehicles
California sys. 2	$1,750	
Colorado	$10,000	Farmers, livestock
Connecticut	No limit	
Delaware	$50	New Castle, Sussex and Kent Counties
District of Columbia	$1625	Artists, mechanics
Florida	None	
Georgia	$1,500	
Hawaii	No limit	
Idaho	$1500	Military
Illinois	$750	
Indiana	No limit	Military
Iowa	$10,000	national guard
Kansas	$7,500	
Kentucky	$300	Farmers, motor vehicles, professionals
Louisiana	No limit	
Maine	$5,000	Farmers, fishing boats
Maryland	$2,500	No car
Massachusetts	$500	Fishing, military
Michigan	$1,000	Military
Minnesota	$13,000	Farmers, teachers
Mississippi	No special allowance	
Missouri	$2,000	
Montana	$3,000	Military, govt. employees
Nebraska	$2,400	
Nevada	$4,500	Farmers, miners, military
New Hampshire	$5,000	Farmers, military
New Jersey	No special allowance	
New Mexico	$1,500	
New York	$600	Military
North Carolina	$750	
North Dakota	No special allowance	
Ohio	$750	
Oklahoma	$5,000	
Oregon	$3,000	
Pennsylvania	1 Sewing machine	
Rhode Island	$1,200	Professionals
South Carolina	$750	
South Dakota	No special allowance	
Tennessee	$1,900	
Texas	No special allowance	
Utah	$3,500	Military
Vermont	$5,000	Nonhouseholders, farmers, military
Virginia	$10,000	Farmers, military
Washington	$5,000	Professionals, farmers
West Virginia	$1,500	
Wisconsin	$7,500	
Wyoming	$2,000	Professionals

Note: Where state has "no special allowance," tools can be kept as part of "personal property" limit.

26 Personal Property

All states and the federal exemptions allow people to keep certain personal property. In some states the amount is just $500 or $1,000, but in most it is $5,000 to $10,000 and in Texas it is $30,000.

In most states, besides a dollar amount you are able to keep specific items regardless of value, such as clothes, furniture, appliances, burial plots, a wedding ring, a Bible, and other similar items supposedly needed to get a fresh start in life.

Because these amounts are small they are not helpful in asset protection. They rarely cover the value of your household effects. This means that if you own valuable personal property such as a coin collection, antique cars or jewelry, you can lose it to your creditors.

In a few states there are no limits on certain items, such as furniture and appliances. Some states allow specific things such as "one watch" or a vehicle equipped for handicapped of unlimited value. In these states you could theoretically refurnish your house with the most expensive furnishings available, have a $50,000 watch and a quarter-million dollar motor home (equipped for your handicap). But as explained elsewhere in this book, it is important not to look like you are greedy and trying to cheat the system. Also, financial transaction in the year and especially the 90 days prior to bankruptcy are looked at carefully and can be voided.

Before shifting into expensive personal property you hope to keep, consult with an experienced bankruptcy attorney.

A rough total of what each state allows is listed in Appendix A. For information on how to research the exact allowances see chapter 49.

27 Alimony & Child Support

In keeping with the policy of protecting income necessary for support, funds received as alimony or child support are exempt from claims of creditors in most states. If you are receiving alimony or child support you do not have to worry that a creditor could garnish or seize the payments.

Like social security and other exempt income, funds received as alimony or support should be put aside into a separate bank account. In some states it is completely exempt so if you can live on other money and just keep setting aside these funds they may be safe from creditors. See Chapter 49 for how to find out exactly what the law is in your state.

What exactly constitutes exempt alimony is an issue that has occasionally reached the courts. One woman who had received over half a million dollars in her divorce settlement filed bankruptcy with her new husband claiming the money as exempt lump sum alimony. Unfortunately for her, the court decided that this money was a division of mutual assets and not the type of alimony which would be exempt. Therefore it was available to pay her creditors' claims. One would expect that the attorney who advised her to file bankruptcy was embarrassed by the court's ruling, though her ex-husband probably received the news with far less sadness in his heart.

28 Public Benefits

In nearly all states public benefits such as unemployment compensation, workers' compensation, veterans' benefits, crime victims' compensation, Aid to Families with Dependent Children (AFDC), aid to the blind and disabled, occupational disease compensation, POWs' benefits, welfare, student aid, relocation benefits, public assistance, or some combination of these is exempt from creditors' claims.

This means that these funds cannot be assigned by a debtor to a creditor. Since these benefits are intended as a safety net for those with no other support, making them available to creditors would defeat the purpose.

Most people using this book will not be concerned with these exemptions. However, if disaster strikes, they may offer useful support while other assets are tied up in a homestead or other exempt property.

29 Other Exemptions

There are other exemptions which do not fall into the previous categories. In some cases they can be quite valuable. Below are a few of them. For information on how to get more specific details, see Chapter 49.

◆ Business partnerships in many states (these are discussed in detail in Chapters 33 and 34). Check your state in Appendix A.

◆ Personal injury recoveries

◆ Wrongful death recoveries

◆ Burial plots

◆ College investment plans

◆ Liquor licenses in Alaska, Idaho, Iowa, Kansas, Oregon and Wyoming

◆ Art curiosities and paleontological remains in Nevada

Part Four - Taking Property Out of Your Name

30 Shifting Property: What's Legal/ What's Not

The key to protecting the most property from your creditors is to have as much of what you own as exempt and as little nonexempt. Any property that cannot be covered by exemptions should be taken out of your name and put into trusts, other entities or family members' names.

There is a wide range of opinion on what shifting of property is legal and what is not. Creditors' attorneys argue that any change in your property which hurts any possible creditor is illegal, while asset protection attorneys argue that only blatant moves to avoid existing creditors are illegal. Depending on your state and court district, the law that applies to you is somewhere in the middle.

One big problem for people with immediate creditor problems is that all transfers within one year of filing a bankruptcy petition must be disclosed and can be set aside by the court. Also, any payments to creditors within 90 days of bankruptcy can be set aside. But if you have no immediate financial problems, you are free to transfer your assets in almost any way which will protect them. The main limitation is that you cannot transfer assets out of your name if to do so will make you insolvent. In states governed by the UFCA rather than the UFTA (see Chapter 4), moving all assets out of your name or converting them to exempt forms can be considered fraudulent.

The common law rule which dates back to the year 1571 is that you cannot transfer property if your intent is to hinder and delay creditors. One big legal issue in asset protection law is whether all asset protection plans fall under this rule, since they are always attempts to defeat some possible future creditors. Fortunately, so far most courts have ruled that if you are not trying to defeat a *specific* creditor at the time of your transfer, the transfer is not fraudulent.

Future creditors can make a successful claim if it appears that a person transferred his assets with plans to do something which might result in liability. For example, there have been cases where people transferred property out of their names and then slandered a partner, killed a girlfriend, or began a hazardous business. In these cases the transfers were found to be fraudulent because the person involved was believed to have already formulated the plan to do wrong when he or she transferred the property.

Future creditors can also make a successful claim if your transfer of assets left you with an unreasonably small amount of capital for the business you are in. For example, if you borrow against all your assets and transfer the funds out of your name so that you have no equity in your business, the transfer can be ruled fraudulent.

The most important factor in deciding whether a transfer was fraudulent is intent. The laws usually use the phrase, "intent to defraud." But intent is something which is in your brain and cannot be seen or proven. A court can only look at the evidence and make its judgment based upon what your intent appeared to be.

A question arises when you have no known creditors at the time you make transfers, but later a claim is made for some act (such as malpractice) which you committed many years earlier but had never previously been brought up. Since the claimant had a "contingent, unliquidated, or unmatured" claim, he or she would come under some definitions of creditor, so it is possible that a court could rule that that creditor was defrauded by a transfer.

One protection against such a possibility is to make all transfers as part of a general estate planning scheme. If you go to an estate planner and say that you want to arrange your affairs to provide for your heirs and your retirement, it will not look like you are intending to defraud any creditors, but are merely doing what is prudent with your estate.

After reading this book you can go to an attorney and you will not have to specifically ask him or her to protect your estate from future creditors. You can simply say you want to provide for your heirs, but then guide the attorney into a plan which you know protects your assets. If a future creditor ever tries to prove you were trying to protect your assets from creditors, your attorney can take the stand and honestly testify that creditors were never mentioned, you only asked for normal estate planning.

This part of the book (Chapters 30 through 41) discusses several ways of protecting your property from creditors. The methods in which you give up all rights to your property (such as a children's trust) are the safest, but they require that you give up control and future enjoyment of the property. The limited liability company, limited partnership and the offshore trust are the best ways available today to protect your assets from creditors but retain control.

Unlike shifting assets from nonexempt to exempt property, transferring property out of your name is not sanctioned by law or by the legislative history. But you do have the freedom to make any transfers you want as long as they are not "fraudulent." As discussed in Chapter 4, certain transfers of property to avoid creditors' claims are considered "fraudulent conveyances" and can be set aside by a court.

31 Making Gifts

As mentioned previously, making a gift is one of the most common means people use to take property out of their names. If done after a creditor has made a claim, it is also one of the least effective and involves the greatest risk of violation of fraudulent transfer laws (Chapter 4). If not made properly, a gift can be seized by a court and sold to pay a creditor.

As usual, the best way to be sure that a gift will be valid is for it to be made before any financial problem arises. It is also possible that a gift made during financial problems can be valid if it is part of a gift-giving plan which was formulated earlier.

For example, if a person gives his children a certain sum each year, then similar sums given during financial problems may be safe from creditors. Estate planning often involves transfers to trusts for life insurance, children or charities. When a program for such giving is set up before problems arise, the gifts are usually safe.

If property is given to fulfill an obligation it is technically not a gift. It is transferred for a valid consideration. Marriage and divorce are times at which this can be done. For example, a gift given to someone in exchange for a promise to marry is considered valid. Also, property given to a spouse in a divorce is not considered a gift, but fulfillment of a valid obligation of support. Such transfers are not fraudulent.

Validity

In order for a gift to be valid, certain legal requirements must be met:

◆ A gift must be intended

◆ The person making the gift must be mentally competent

◆ The property must be delivered

◆ The property must be accepted

◆ The gift must be complete (no retained interest)

If you "give" your Rolex watch to your son but then continue to wear it and treat it as your own, it may not be legally considered to have been made a gift. (Can you believe that some debtors have actually gone into bankruptcy court wearing such a watch and giving such an explanation!) In some states, when a gift is made but the property is not transferred, the gift is presumed to be fraudulent. Another rule of making gifts is that if property is transferred to a "natural object of a person's bounty," such as a child or spouse, then it is presumed to be a gift.

Of course, as in most areas of law, there are no black and white rules as to when a gift fails to meet legal requirements. Each case stands or falls on its own circumstances and sometimes on who the judge has the most sympathy for. Some exceptions to the above rules have been made when minor children were involved, when the property was loaned back, when there was a trust, or when a life estate had been created.

Taxes

When making gifts, tax aspects must be kept in mind. Under federal gift tax law a person is allowed to give $11,000 per year tax free to any person, but any amount over that may be taxed. In addition to the $11,000 exemption, gifts of $1,000,000 are allowed over a lifetime and subtracted from the exclusion at death. If you are contemplating gifts of over $11,000 per person per year you should consult a competent tax advisor.

Spouses

Probably the most common practice of people attempting to avoid creditors is to put property into a spouse's name. This practice has two problems. The first problem is that since 50% of marriages end in divorce, putting your property in your spouse's name may cost you all of the property in the end anyway. If your divorce is nasty you would probably rather have your property go to your creditor than to your spouse.

Many people who think their marriages are perfectly stable find to their dismay that their spouse has gotten bored and found someone new. This is especially common for the successful male. As Dr. Warren Farrell points out in his book, *Why Men Are the Way They Are*, women are most interested in men who are extremely successful, but then many aren't happy with them because those men devote so much time to their professions. They then divorce the successful one, taking half the assets, and find a more nurturing man.

If you put property in the name of your spouse to protect it from creditors, be sure that in case of divorce you have evidence to prove that you were not making a gift. This could be a statement on a deed or other writing stating that a transfer is being made "not as a gift, but for estate planning purposes only."

In some states, if a piece of property owned by one party is put in joint names it is presumed to be a gift to the other party. If you transfer property to your spouse be sure you have some paperwork to show that it was done for "estate planning" purposes and not as a gift.

The second problem with putting property in the name of a spouse is that the transfer can be challenged by creditors. Under bankruptcy and fraudulent conveyance laws property transferred without fair payment after a creditor has appeared can be set aside.

In some states you can title property in the names of both a husband and wife and it will be untouchable by creditors. As explained is Chapter 20 tenancy by the entireties is a legal concept in which the title to the property is considered to be owned by the married couple as a couple and the claims of just one of them cannot touch it. Only about half the states clearly recognize the concept of tenancy by the entireties property and not all of those protect the property from creditors. But if you are lucky enough to live in a state which does, then anything you title this way can be protected from the creditors of one spouse (but not creditors of both spouses). See Chapter 20.

When using tenancy by the entireties you must be careful to be sure that all property you intend to be titled this way actually is. Unless property is clearly titled this way a court may rule that creditors can take it. You should have written documentation for all property indicating that it is so titled.

Some banks have signature cards which do not adequately provide for tenancy by the entireties and such accounts could be seized by creditors. You should review the account agreement for each of your bank accounts and be sure that it is an entireties account. If not, you should instruct your bank in writing to change your account and to acknowledge that they have done so. If they refuse to, you can switch to a more knowledgeable bank.

Children

Putting property into the names of your children is an excellent way to protect it from the claims of your creditors as long as you realize that this property becomes an irrevocable gift to the children. If you have property that you intend for their education or that you are sure you will never need again then you can transfer it permanently into their names or into a trust for them and it will be unreachable by your creditors. However, if you are afraid they will not be able to handle the money themselves, or if you think that you might need the property in the future, this is not a good idea.

To put property in the names of children who are still minors you can set up bank accounts or other investments under the Uniform Gifts to Minors Act which can protect assets from creditors and also reduce your income taxes. Keep in mind, however, that at the age of 18 (21 in some states) a minor has the right to full control of the funds to set aside and you have only whatever power of persuasion you have managed to retain over the child.

When considering putting property into your children's names, you must also consider the risk that the children themselves may have creditor problems. Even if their occupations are not as risky as yours, they may be involved in an auto accident or other incident which would result in liability. Fortunately, there is an easy solution to this. If you make the gift in the form of a spendthrift trust, the funds can be used to benefit the children and still be out of reach of their creditors. See Chapter 36 on children's trusts for more information.

32 Limited Liability Companies

The limited liability company is one of the best asset protection devices ever to be developed and it has only been available for the last few years. No asset protection plan should be without at least one limited liability company. More advanced plans should have several of them.

A limited liability company is a newly created business entity, similar to a corporation, but simpler and usually cheaper. It has been described as a limited partnership but without needing a general partner. (For more information on limited partnerships and general partnerships see the next two chapters.)

The beauty of a limited liability company is that in many states it offers double asset protection. Both a corporation and a limited liability company protect you from business liabilities. That is, as the owner of either of these entities you are not liable for the debts of the business or acts of employees. But the LLC offers the extra protection that if you do something wrong personally, for example, you kill someone while driving your car, the victim cannot take your LLC away from you. He can take your corporation away from you just like he can take any stock you own that is not exempt. But your ownership interest in an LLC, if it is set up right, cannot be taken.

The law adopted by many states for setting up limited liability companies was based on limited partnership law. Under these laws, the creditor of a limited partner cannot seize a limited partnership interest because it would disrupt the business. All the creditor gets is a charging order, which is like a claim or lien against the interest. This lien cannot be foreclosed, it just sits there at the mercy of the other partners.

The worst thing (for the creditor, it is good for the debtor) is that a creditor with a charging order against an LLC might have to pay taxes on the income of the business even though he has no way to get at the income!

Unfortunately, not all states offer this protection. However, if your state does not, you can form an LLC in a state with more favorable laws. See page 152 for a list of state LLC laws.

Another good thing is that in many states the annual fee to keep an LLC active is very low, in some states as low as $10 or even $5. The formation fees are usually no more than $100 or $200 so at these prices anyone can afford several LLCs.

A good plan is to use one LLC for your business, to separate risks from yourself. Most lawyers today feel it is foolish to operate a business that is not an LLC or a corporation. Then you can use another LLC to hold your assets. In fact you can put different assets in different LLCs. Many real estate investors put each property they own in a separate LLC.

One important thing to know about using LLCs to protect your assets from creditors is that it may be necessary to have at least two members of the LLC to have the protection from members' creditors, depending on how your state's LLC law is written. In a recent case a court denied protection to LLC assets where there was only one member. *In re: Albright*, Case No. 01-11367, April 4, 2003, United States Bankruptcy Court, District of Colorado.

If you have a close family member you wish to share the property with you can be equal owners with that person. If you don't wish to share quite so much, you can assign the person a small amount, 5%, 2%, possibly just 1% and still be protected from creditors. A local attorney who specializes in business law can advise you as to what is prudent in your state.

(Since LLCs are relatively new many attorneys stay away from them and prefer to form corporations which they have been doing for years. Find an attorney who knows about and likes the LLC.)

If you are normally a one person operation without family members you can bring in, you may be able to use a corporation or another LLC as the member of your LLC in order to have two members. In a tough lawsuit, it is possible a judge could nix such a plan if it was not set up right or was abused, but under the law this should be possible.

Another great aspect of an LLC is that you don't have to pay taxes according to your ownership. You can allocate profits and losses different from ownership. In fact one owner can get the profits and another the losses in some cases. See your tax expert for this type of planning.

As mentioned earlier, the LLC is a new legal development. The good thing about this is that no one knows how courts will look at each aspect of their operation, so lawyers may face delays in attacking them. The bad thing about this is that we can't be 100% sure about the outcome. But the purpose of the statutes is clear and in most cases the LLC should be successful in its intended purpose of protecting assets.

There are two basic types of LLC statutes regarding the rights of creditors. Both say the creditor can get a charging order but some say that this is the exclusive remedy. Where this is not the exclusive remedy, a creditor may be able to foreclose his lien on the member's interest. But then his rights may only be those of an assignee, which under the statute or under the agreement, may be almost none unless the other members agree.

In two states, Nebraska and Pennsylvania, there is not a specific limitation of the creditor's rights to a charging order. However, since their laws provide that a transferee of an interest has almost no rights, the creditor would not be much better off than in the other states.

LLC Statutes on Creditor's Rights

Alabama	10-12-35(a)	Missouri	347.119
Alaska	10.50.380	Montana	35-8-705
Arizona	29-655	Nevada	86.401
Arkansas	4-32-705	New Hampshire	304C:47
California	17302	New Jersey	42:2B-45
Colorado	7-80-703	New Mexico	53-19-35
Connecticut	34-171	New York	34-607
Delaware	18-703	North Carolina	57C-5-03
D.C.	29-1338	North Dakota	10-32-34
Florida	608.433	Ohio	1705.19
Georgia	14-11-504	Oklahoma	18-32-2034
Idaho	53-637	Oregon	7-63.259
Illinois	30-20	Rhode Island	7-16-37
Indiana	23-18-6-7	South Carolina	33-44-504
Iowa	490A.904	South Dakota	47-34A-504
Kansas	17-76,113	Tennessee	48-218-105
Kentucky	275.260	Texas	4.06
Louisiana	1331	Utah	48-2C-1103
Maine	686	Vermont	21-3074
Maryland	4A-607	Virginia	13.1-1041
Massachusetts	22-156C-40	Washington	25.15.255
Michigan	450.4507	West Virginia	31B-5-504
Minnesota	322B.32	Wisconsin	183.0705
Mississippi	79-29-703	Wyoming	17-15-145

Offshore Limited Liability Companies

Since limited liability companies appear to be one of the most successful asset protection devices at the moment, some promoters have attempted to make them even more effective by setting them up offshore. One promoter who insists offshore trusts are nearly worthless suggests offshore LLCs are better.

Since one problem with offshore trusts is that they look bad and might influence a judge or jury to break them just because of their reputation, it is hard to see why an offshore LLC would look any better. However, as part of an estate plan for a large estate (as opposed to tax fraud) an offshore LLC may offer needed protection.

An offshore LLC would clearly be harder to break than a local LLC. As long as the assets were offshore, the creditor would have to go to that jurisdiction and hire a local lawyer to file a lawsuit there.

For extra protection the manager of an offshore LLC could be another LLC in another offshore location. You could own 99% of the first LLC and the manager, another LLC could own 1%. Even if you gave your 99% to your creditor (and looked like a good guy to the court), he could do nothing with it. And while he is trying to figure out what to do, the assets of the LLC could be dribbled away.

Not all foreign LLC laws are created equal, and of course they change. At the present Nevis (in the Caribbean) has one of the best laws with the "charging order" provision which protects the assets. There are several companies that set them up for under $1,000. There is a list of providers located here:

http://www.worldoffshorebanks.com/stkittspro.html

The a good analysis of offshore LLCs, see Riser, Chris, *Riser's Guide to Offshore Limited Liability Companies.*

Starting an LLC

It is very simple to start an LLC in any state. Usually you just need to file a short form called Articles of Organization or a similar name. In most states you can do this on-line. However, you should also have an Operating Agreement or a Management Agreement and become familiar with your state's laws regarding the operation of an LLC.

There are a few books on the market explaining how to start and run an LLC. Three which were written by the author of this book are:

How to Form a Limited Liability Company
(This book explains how to form an LLC in all 50 states)

How to Form a Limited Liability Company in Florida
This is an LLC book just for Florida

Limited Liability Company Forms Book—An LLC Operating Manual
(This book includes over 100 form for the day-to-day operation of an LLC. It is due out in January, 2004)

These books are available through the publisher of this book (see last page) or from major bookstores and Internet book sellers. Be sure to get the latest edition.

You can of course have an attorney set up your LLC and this is the best way to get good legal guidance for your specific situation. However, be sure the attorney you choose is knowledgable about LLCs. (You may be able to get an honest answer by calling the attorney's secretary and asking if they have set up many limited liability companies.)

After meeting clients who had their LLCs set up incorrectly by attorneys for $800 and more, the author started offering to set up Florida LLCs for $300 plus costs through his company, Land Trust Service Corporation. For more information, see www.floridalandtrust.com

33 General Partnerships

In most states, property of business partnerships is exempt from creditors (check your state in Appendix B). If you file for bankruptcy owning an interest in a general partnership, the property of the partnership cannot be used to pay your debts. However, for asset protection purposes, general partnerships are not a good idea, and in most cases are very dangerous.

The biggest problem with general partnerships is that each partner is liable for acts of all other partners done in the scope of the business. If you are in a general partnership with other professionals, you can be personally liable if one of them gets into an auto accident while on business, defrauds someone through the business, sexually harasses an employee, or injures a client or patient.

One way to protect against liability for other partners' acts is for each partner to form a corporation and then have the corporations form a partnership. This is done by many attorneys and medical professionals. This protects the partner's personal assets from partnership claims. However, all of the assets of the corporation are subject to claims against the partnership, and the stock in the corporation itself may be seized by your personal creditors.

This is not a problem if the corporation has few assets. However, if a lot of assets are necessary for the business other devices must be used to protect them.

The best way to protect them is to have them owned by a separate corporation or trust and then to lease them. This can have tax advantages such as when the assets are owned by a children's trust. Money which would have been given to the children anyway for education expenses can be deducted as a lease payment for equipment of the business!

Another way to protect the corporation which is the partner in the business is to have its stock owned by one's children or spouse. Of course the usefulness of this setup depends upon the potential for problems within the family. Also, in some states stockholders of some professional corporations must be licensed in the profession.

34 Limited Partnerships

The limited partnership can be an important method of protecting assets. This is because the laws in all 50 states protect partnership assets from the claims (unrelated to the business) against one partner. This protection is available because it would be unfair to other partners to have the partnership dissolved, or property seized, for acts over which they had no control.

When used for asset protection purposes, a limited partnership is usually called a family limited partnership. Until limited liability companies came along limited partnerships and offshore trusts were the two most successful asset protection devices available. Now you have three possibilities

There has been an ongoing war between promoters of limited partnerships and foreign trusts as to what is better. Of course each argues that the other doesn't work. So far no courts have clearly abandoned the protections offered by limited partnerships, and any judicial abandonment would probably take many years to accomplish. Promoters of limited partnerships rightly point out that they have worked in protecting assets for nearly a hundred years while foreign trusts and limited liability companies are relatively recent.

The few cases which ruled against limited partnerships applied to very narrow, unusual situations. At present, limited partnerships are very successful in protecting assets from creditors' claims. Even Federal Deposit Insurance Corporation claims against bank directors have been abandoned when it was discovered that all their assets were in limited partnerships.

Lawyers make money getting quick settlements, not litigating for years in hope of changing the law. Therefore, a limited partnership would be a successful roadblock to most claims. Even if the lawyer thought he had a chance to win in the end, few would invest the time or money involved in the appeals necessary to change the law.

What a Limited Partnership Is

A limited partnership is a partnership agreement between two or more persons in which at least one of them (the limited partner) has no right to control the business and no liability for debts of the partnership. The general partner (or partners) controls the business or assets and is liable for the partnership debts. The limited partners own a share but have no say in the operation. They can share in the profits according to their percentage ownership if the general partner decides to distribute profits.

Why the Limited Partnership Works

The reason that a limited partnership works is that a creditor of a person who owns an interest in a limited partnership cannot seize the interest or the property owned by the partnership. All he can do is obtain a "charging order" which is a lien against the limited partnership interest. The charging order only entitles the creditor to any profits distributed to the partner. But in a family limited partnership, the general partner can decide not to distribute any profits.

But the biggest drawback to the creditor is that if he obtains a charging lien he may have to pay a share of the taxes on the profits of the limited partnership even if no profits are distributed! This means he can go for years paying taxes but receiving nothing. Needless to say, few creditors want to obtain charging liens against limited partnerships.

Besides owning part of the limited partnership interests, you could also own a 1% interest as the sole general partner, which would give you complete control over the assets of the partnership. While some lawyers feel that this ownership could be a problem in bankruptcy, most partnerships are set up so that if you, as the general partner, face a financial problem you can resign or be automatically replaced as general partner.

Tax Advantage

The family limited partnership also offers a terrific estate tax advantage. When a business or other asset is put in a limited partnership, it is worth less than it would be if it were not in a limited partnership. This is because none of the partners has complete control. This lower value can mean lower estate taxes and the ability to give greater gifts each year under the $11,000 exclusion.

Some estates may even avoid estate taxes. If assets valued at $1,200,000 are put in a limited partnership and the value is then discounted 30%, the $840,000 value would be under the $1,000,000 threshold for filing an estate tax return. Discounts can go as high as 40% depending on how the ownership is set up. But this is a complicated and changing area of tax law so you need an experienced tax expert to be sure to do it legally.

Ways to Use a Limited Partnership

There are several ways a limited partnership can be used to protect assets. A person can have one partnership or several. Here are several examples of how limited partnerships can be used:

◆ A couple could put all of their investments into a limited partnership and then give $11,000 worth of shares to each family member each year. This would transfer interests tax-free to the family before death, but the husband or wife or both could keep complete control of the assets until their deaths and decide whether or not to distribute actual cash.

◆ A person could put his business, his investments and his apartment building each in a separate limited partnership. That way, if the business or apartment building had any liability problem it would not affect other assets. In some cases it would be better to make one partnership a subsidiary of the other, in others it would not.

◆ A single person could put his antiques collection into a limited partnership in which he owned the 1% general partnership interest and 94% of the limited partnership interest. His children or parents could own the other 5% limited partnership interest. If he were sued for some reason his partnership interest could be made subject to a charging lien, but the antiques could not be seized by his creditor.

◆ The limited partnership interests can be put into a living trust to avoid probate. For large estates, a trust could be set up for each spouse (A-B trusts) which would allow the children to inherit $2,000,000 tax-free ($1,000,000 from each spouse).

◆ For extra protection the limited partnership interest could be put into an offshore trust.

Necessary Provisions

To set up a limited partnership a certificate of limited partnership must be filed with the Secretary of State in the state in which it will be located. When setting up a limited partnership for asset protection purposes, the following provisions are important:

◆ The interests should not be transferable.

◆ A person obtaining an interest through foreclosure or bankruptcy should not be able to become a partner without the unanimous consent of other partners.

◆ The partnership should not be able to liquidate without the consent of all partners

◆ The right of a partner to withdraw should be limited

◆ The general partner should be replaced immediately by a named successor if he ever files bankruptcy.

◆ Death, bankruptcy or disability of a partner should not cause liquidation of the partnership.

◆ Distributions to partners should be limited.

◆ Redemption of a partner's interest should be provided for.

◆ The partnership should be set up for a set term of years (which can be extended).

◆ The partnership should be properly set up so that it is not taxed as a corporation.

Operation

To be sure not to lose the protections of the partnership, it should always be operated as a separate entity.

◆ Partnership funds should be kept separate from personal funds.

◆ All dealings with the partnership should be formal and at arm's length.

◆ Separate books and records should be kept for the partnership.

◆ File partnership tax returns.

Drawbacks

Nothing in life is free and there is a cost for everything, including limited partnerships. The biggest drawback to the limited partnership is the cost. There are attorney fees for formation, annual registration fees, and accounting fees for the limited partnership tax return. However, in most cases the tax savings and advantages will outweigh the costs.

In states which have high annual fees for limited partnerships, it may be possible to use a limited partnership registered in another state. If that state does not require a registered office your fees there could be minimal. And if the partnership holds investments, rather than conducting an active business, you might not have to pay the fees in your state.

The next best thing to a limited partnership is a limited liability company. In most states it has the same advantages. The only drawback is that it hasn't been around as long. Promoters of limited partnerships use this fact to sell their (much more expensive) product. However, there is no reason to believe that courts won't follow the clear intent of LLC laws to protect the assets.

Set Up

Unfortunately, limited partnerships are not as easy as corporations and LLCs to set up. To be sure to do it right an attorney should be consulted. One book that was recently published on limited partnerships is *Family Limited Partnership: How to Protect Your Family Business and Provide for Your Children* by Karen Ann Rolcik.

35 Living Trusts

Living trusts are used by millions of Americans to keep their assets from going through probate. However, most living trusts are not good for protecting assets from creditors because they are revocable. This means that the person setting up the trust can revoke or change the terms of the trust at any time. If a trust is revocable, and a person can get control of the assets in the trust at any time, the courts have consistently held that that person's creditors can also get control of the assets.

There are ways to incorporate living trusts into an asset protection scheme, and some asset protection planners use them. But these are usually used in conjunction with limited partnerships or offshore trusts.

One situation in which living trusts could be useful for asset protection is where a couple in a stable marriage wished to divide their property equally to avoid claims against one spouse who is in a risky profession. In such a scenario each spouse sets up a living trust providing lifetime income to him- or herself, with the remainder to the children. The exempt property is put in the trust of the at-risk spouse and the nonexempt property is put in the other spouse's trust. This arrangement can provide protection which is similar to tenancy by the entireties property in states which do not recognize the concept.

Husband-wife living trusts, also known as A-B trusts, can also avoid estate taxes by allowing both spouses to take advantage of the $1,000,000 lifetime exclusion. In this arrangement each spouse has a separate trust which allows both spouses to pass $1,000,000 to the next generation (or other beneficiaries) tax-free.

Two good sources for information on living trusts are:

Rolcik, Karen Ann, *Living trusts and Other Ways to Avoid Probate*, Sphinx Publishing, $24.95

Clifford, Denis, *Make Your Own Living Trust*, Nolo Press, $39.99

Irrevocable Trusts

Trusts can be more successfully used to protect assets if they are irrevocable. This means that once you set them up you cannot change the terms. Since you cannot revoke them or change the terms, your creditors cannot either, and the property in them is safe. These types of trusts are discussed further in the following chapters.

36 Children's Trusts

If you have children to whom you wish to give part of your assets, a children's trust can offer both tax savings and asset protection. If you have young children, such a trust can offer three benefits. Once your property is transferred to such a trust it can no longer be reached by your creditors, it is no longer part of your estate, and at least some of the income can be taxed at the children's lower rates. This trust is usually called a "2503C" trust, after the tax code provision which covers it.

Such a trust is a good way to set aside funds which will be used for a child's education. If you plan on paying those expenses anyway, you can allow the funds to accumulate interest at a lower tax rate and keep them safe from your creditors.

A creative way to use the trust is to use the funds in the trust to purchase equipment which you need in your business. The trust can then lease these items to your business and the lease payments (which you would have given to your children for education expenses anyway) are tax deductible!

However, one aspect of the children's trust which must be stressed is that once property has been transferred to the trust it cannot be taken back. Absolute control must be surrendered and once the children reach legal age they can do what they want with the assets. While you may have intended the funds to go for education expenses your children may be more interested in clothes, cars, or drugs. One parent got a call from his daughter at a commune in California demanding to receive $50,000 from her trust on her upcoming 21st birthday. He was told that if it was not sent, he would hear from the commune's lawyer.

Legal age depends on state law and can range from 18 to 25. Parents can choose between setting up the trust in the state where the trustee is located, or the state where the donor or the child resides. Choosing the state with the highest legal age allows the parents to maintain control of the trust until the child is more mature. This does not guarantee the child will be ready to make financial decisions when the time comes, but a few years delay may help.

When a child reaches legal age it is possible to extend the trust until a later age with the child's written consent. However, not all children are cooperative at this age and some may be tempted to take the money immediately. One possibility is to threaten to cut off all future financial connections, but even this may not sway a child at that age.

Setting up the trust when a child is young allows a greater period of interest accumulation. However, at this time it is too early to tell if the child will be able to make the right decisions at the age of majority. For this reason some parents wait until a later age to set up the trust. When the child reaches fourteen, the tax law allows all income of the trust to be taxed to the child, which is another advantage because the child's tax rate is lower.

Income from the trust cannot be used to pay for necessities of the child, but can be used for other items such as vacations, uniforms, music lessons and summer camp. If the tax law is not carefully followed there could be penalties; however, this item is not one which is carefully scrutinized by the IRS.

Some other aspects of the children's trust are as follows:

◆ The trustee should not be you, your employee, or a close relative.

◆ Assets you give to the trust cannot be sold within the first two years.

◆ Until the age of 14, the first $1,200 in income in the trust is taxed at the child's rate and any above that at the parent's rate.

◆ At age 14, the income is all taxed at the child's rate.

To set up a children's trust you should check with your tax advisor and an attorney who specializes in this area. Some advisors feel that you can obtain similar benefits more easily with a family limited partnership set up for the children's benefit.

37 Charitable Remainder Trusts

While giving your assets to charity may not sound like a good way to protect them for yourself, under the amazing American system of taxation you can give away your property and enjoy it too. Americans give about five times as much to charities as the French and about three times as much as the British. The reason is our tax code.

The most useful device is the Charitable Remainder Trust or CRT. Using a CRT you can give away property but retain an income stream for life and have the value of the property go to your heirs. Sounds too good to be true? It works best for those in the highest tax brackets, but it also works for others. Here is how:

Suppose you have stock worth $100,000 which you bought years ago for $30,000. If you sold it to invest in Treasury bonds for retirement income, you would pay about $21,000 income tax on the profit, and upon your death (if you are in the highest tax bracket) another $44,000 in tax would be due, leaving your heirs with only $36,000 from the original $100,000 value.

Instead of selling the stock, you could give it to a Charitable Remainder Trust. As part of the deal you could require that you receive the same income that you would have gotten on Treasury bonds for the rest of your life. You not only get to deduct the donation as a gift, but with the tax savings you can buy life insurance which will give your heirs more than the $36,000 they would have received if you had followed the above example. This way you get the same income, your heirs get an even better inheritance than they would have, and you get a tax deduction.

This is a simplification of the issues. There are formulas for figuring the deductions and how much income may be received. But the CRT works quite well, especially with property which has appreciated in value since you bought it.

A charitable trust can be set up as either a Charitable Remainder Annuity Trust (CRAT) or a Charitable Remainder Unitrust (CRU).

Internal Revenue Code §664 provides the rules for setting up charitable trusts. Sample forms are contained in Revenue Rulings 89-20, 89-21, 90-30 and 90-32. However, these laws are quite complicated so it is advisable to work with a qualified tax advisor or attorney.

38 Domestic Asset Protection Trusts

Asset protection trusts have been around for a long time and they have worked in certain situations. But new laws have been passed making them even more useful. While the newness of the laws make them open to challenge, the legal basis seems strong enough to work if the trusts are not clearly abusive.

Spendthrift Trusts

Spendthrift trusts are trusts which contain clauses which prevent the beneficiaries or their creditors from getting to the assets of the trust. They have been used for many years and have been very successful. Most states recognize and enforce spendthrift trusts.

An example would be a trust that is set up for a child who cannot control his spending. If the trust is set up to pay him a certain amount each month, with no right to get any more or to assign the payments to anyone, it would be a spendthrift trust and could not be reached by the child's creditors. However, in many states, once payments were made to the child the creditor could reach them. For further protection, the trust could be set up to make payments for the benefit of the beneficiary, for example to pay his rent, food bills, etc. directly to the providers instead of to the beneficiary.

One problem with spendthrift trusts for asset protection planning is that American courts have always ruled that a person cannot set up a spendthrift trust for his own benefit. Also, two people cannot set up spendthrift trusts for each other. Therefore, if you wish to set up a spendthrift trust you must make it for the benefit of someone else and forever give up control of the property.

If you wish to provide for your spouse, parents, children or other person dear to you this may be a useful way to insure that gifts to them are not taken by your creditors. Children's trusts are discussed in the Chapter 36 and similar trusts can be set up for other persons' benefit.

In some states there is a way to set up a trust in which you can retain some benefit. If you set up an irrevocable trust in which you will receive the income for life and the remainder will go to others, such as your spouse and children, the property in the trust will be safe from your creditors (though it will still be considered part of your estate for tax purposes). However, if the income is paid directly to you, it can be reached by your creditors. To avoid this it can be paid directly to those who provide you with food, shelter or other items.

One way which might protect the income from your creditors would be to make it solely for your health, support and maintenance, solely at the discretion of the trustee, and only if it did not jeopardize the amounts payable to the other beneficiaries. Such an arrangement requiring loss of control of one's assets is usually not desirable.

Self-Settled Asset Protection Trusts

Beginning in 1997, a few states saw the opportunity to improve their economy by allowing nonresidents to set up asset protection trusts under their jurisdictions. This is similar to the situation over a hundred years ago when Delaware first simplified its laws for forming corporations and other states eventually followed suit. So far, Alaska, Delaware, Nevada, and Rhode Island have passed laws allowing these types of trusts.

Because they are so new, no one can predict how they will hold up in court. Creditors' attorneys argue that they can't possibly work and are a bad joke, while asset protection attorneys argue that if set up properly for the right reasons they can work just as the laws provide.

So far there have been no big cases involving these trusts so it is too early to tell how they will be interpreted by the courts. However, if you have a large estate to protect, you should consider using one as at least part of your asset protection plan.

The laws setting up these asset protection trusts were carefully written to protect assets without being subject to abuse. For example, the Nevada law does not give full protection until the trust has been set up for two years and Delaware law requires four years. This means you can't use these trusts if you already have a claim pending against you. The Nevada law protects the assets from alimony and child support, but the Delaware law does not.

Some tips for protecting your asset protection trust from attack:

- ◆ The trustees should all be in the state where the trust is set up, not in your home state. This is so your state won't have jurisdiction over the trustee.

- ◆ The trust should state that it is being set up under the law of the state where it is set up. This so a court won't use your state's law.

- ◆ The trust should be executed in the state where the trust is set up and you should have a bank account there. Again, to build a connection with the other state.

- ◆ You should have as little control as possible over the distributions from the trust.

- ◆ The trust should be set up as soon as possible, as far in advance of any risk as is possible.

- ◆ These trusts are most likely to work for residents of the states where they are set up.

To set up a domestic asset protection trust you need to work with a company which offers them in one of the four states listed. Keep in mind that a trustee has full control of your property so be sure to deal only with a reputable company.

The biggest argument against asset protection trusts is that your local court doesn't have to follow the law of the state where your trust is located and that once there is a judgment against you and your trust the asset protection state has to honor the judgment of another state.

One big question with this scenario is whether they could get jurisdiction of the trustee. The answer may depend on whether the trustee advertised nationally or had a web site!

But the best solution would be for a debtor to file suit in the asset protection state to have it declared that a creditor could not get it. Then all other states would have to honor that judgment from the asset protection state. The key is to race to the courthouse as soon as you know you have a creditor.

39 Offshore Asset Protection Trusts

The foreign, or offshore trust was one of the hottest asset protection techniques about a decade ago. Several small nations, at the request of U. S. lawyers passed laws allowing Americans (an others) to set up trusts in their countries which under their new laws were safe from nearly all creditors.

At $20,000 to $30,000 a pop, U.S. law firms raked in tons of money setting up these trusts and numerous American millionaires slept easier, until some of the trusts were taken to court. The first case was the Anderson case, *FTC v. Affordable Media LLC*, 179 F.3d 1228 (9th Cir. 1999), in which a couple obtained several million dollars through a Ponzi scheme and put it in a Cook Islands trust. When they said they couldn't get the money back they were put in prison and spent six months there until they appointed the FTC trustee and beneficiary of the trust.

The second big blow to foreign asset protection trusts was the Lawrence case, *In re Stephen J. Lawrence*, 238 B.R. 498 (S.D. Fla. Bankr. 1999) in which Mr. Lawrence was fined $10,000 a day and sent to federal prison for not bringing his money back from his foreign trust.

In a third case, *SEC v. Bilzerian*, 131 F. Supp. 2d 10 (2001) Mr. Bilzerian was also ordered to prison for not complying with orders to bring back the money and provide a copy of the Cook Islands trust.

Besides the cases, negative sentiment from some legal scholars against foreign trusts is quite strong. At least two law review articles suggested that it should be made a crime to set up a foreign asset protection trust. Gingiss, R., Putting a Stop to "Asset Protection" Trusts, 51 Baylor L. Rev. 987 (1999), and Sterk, S., Asset Protection Trusts: Trust Law's Race to the Bottom, 85 Cornell L. Rev. 1036 (2000)

The biggest problem with offshore asset protection trusts is that they look shady. They look like just a trick to get away with not paying legal creditors. Judges really don't like tricks, and often they will stretch the law to get someone who has tried to use a trick.

In the Lawrence case the judge said, "…it defies reason—it tortures reason—to accept and believe that this debtor transferred over $7 million in 1991, an amount representing over 90% of his liquid net worth, to a trust in a far away place administered by a stranger…"

After the above cases some attorneys said that offshore trusts are dead, they obviously can't work any more. But others argued that these were three extreme cases where debtors were very blatant, made transfers after judgments were entered, and appeared to be thumbing their noses at the court. If an offshore trust were set up as part of a long term estate plan by someone with no current liabilities, some argue it would likely hold up.

In the three cases, the trusts actually worked in that the creditors couldn't get the money. But the debtors went to prison. If a debtor were to move out of the country this wouldn't happen. And some argue that if some of those debtors hadn't filed bankruptcy and tried to deceive the bankruptcy courts they would not have gone to prison.

As explained elsewhere in the book, the best asset protection plan is one that is diversified. If you have assets under several different types of protections, it is likely at least some of them will work. If you have a multi-million dollar estate then you may want to put part of it in an offshore trust.

Uses and Benefits of Offshore Trusts

The liability crisis in this country has been noted around the world and many of the banks handling offshore trusts are well established and in some cases safer than American banks.

Because of the reputation of foreign havens which have been used to hide ill-gotten funds from drug operations, most legitimate asset protection companies today are extremely careful in their dealing with Americans. They require references and clear evidence that their clients are not involved in illegal activities. Many require a personal interview.

In previous years, foreign trusts were used by the wealthy to avoid paying U. S. income tax. However, recent laws have eliminated the tax savings from foreign trusts. As explained later in this chapter, these trusts are now tax-neutral. Yet in the last few years countless Americans have begun using foreign trusts in several jurisdictions.

Years ago most people setting up offshore trusts were residents of countries that ran the risk of political strife and coup d'etat, such as Third World dictatorships. Many of them set up their trusts in the United States. It is a sad commentary on the state of our nation that it is now Americans who must send their assets abroad for protection!

Foreign trusts offer many benefits, some of which are traditional trust benefits and others of which are only available overseas. Among these are:

◆ Privacy
◆ Diversification of assets
◆ Avoidance of probate
◆ Qualification for entitlements such as Medicaid

◆Avoidance of the need for a premarital agreement
◆Avoidance of forced heirship laws
◆Protection from seizure by creditors

To understand the asset protection benefits of a foreign trust over a U. S. trust, consider the following. In the U. S. a person suing you has a certain period of time (i.e. two or four years, depending on the state and the court) from the time *he finds out you set up a trust* to try to set it aside. In some countries the person has two years from the date you *set up the trust*. If the person does not have a claim against you until five years after you set up the foreign trust there is nothing he can do.

Next, suppose the person has filed suit against you in the U.S., and after three years of litigation has won a judgment. Most likely he won't find out about your foreign trust until after he has obtained his judgment. If he then wants to try to seize your foreign trust he must file his suit all over again in the country where your trust is located. To do so he must hire a lawyer in that country. Unlike in the U.S., the lawyers in the country where you set up your trust cannot work on a percentage basis, but must charge by the hour. Then, in the unlikely event he could win the same case under the laws of that country he would have to file another suit to try to set aside your trust. In that case the burden would be on the creditor to prove that you specifically intended to defraud *him* years ago when you set up the trust. Meanwhile, your trustee has resigned and transferred the trust to another country. So your creditor has to start all over in the new country! If not foolproof, this adventure is more than most American lawyers would like to pursue.

While this can be a drawback for other reasons, one of the best things about the foreign trust is that there is so much uncertainty and few lawyers know much about them. While a collections lawyer might be eager to seize your bank account and your car, he may have no idea how to begin collecting from a foreign trust. When he considers the cost of hiring another lawyer to help him, especially in a foreign country, and the fact that he must pay in advance, win or lose, he may settle for pennies on the dollar or just give up.

Important Characteristics

The following are the characteristics usually used in a successful offshore asset protection trust:

- ◆ Independent Foreign Trustee. The grantor of the trust should never be the trustee, and the trustee should not have any offices or branches in the United States. In some cases it may be advisable to have a U.S. co-trustee (mostly for tax reasons), but he should resign or be removed in the event of financial trouble of the grantor.

- ◆ Beneficiaries. Attorneys are divided on whether a person setting up a trust may be a beneficiary. Some suggest that a creditor might be able to reach the trust if the person was beneficiary. Others say that foreign laws would bar creditors from making claims and that the whole point of the trust is to protect assets while keeping the benefits. The best position seems to be that the person setting up the trust can be a "discretionary" beneficiary and a "contingent remainder" beneficiary as explained in the next two paragraphs.

- ◆ All Disbursements Discretionary. The money paid out of the trust by the trustee should be solely at the trustee's discretion. No one can force the trustee to distribute any funds except as provided for in the trust document. This is because if you could demand distribution, your creditor could also demand distributions. You may be afraid to give a trustee total discretion over what to disburse to you. However, as one trust officer explained to the author, "We have total discretion over what to disburse, however, we take your wishes into consideration." In other words, if you phone the trustee and say that you need a disbursement, it will be done.

◆ Remainder. The trust provides that it will dissolve either upon the death of the grantor or after a set number of years. The term of years could be extended by the grantor, and if the grantor were in financial trouble, the trust would be extended automatically. If the grantor were alive at the termination of the trust, the assets could go to him, or if the trust terminated upon his death, they would go to remainder beneficiaries whom he named. Since the grantor might get the assets back if he lives longer than the term of the trust, he is a "contingent beneficiary."

◆ Right to Change Beneficiaries. The grantor of the trust can retain the right to change the beneficiaries who are to get the property upon his death.

◆ Jurisdiction. The country chosen for the trust must be one which has laws specifically protecting such trusts. Such countries have recently passed laws which make it difficult for creditors to attack such a trust. Some of the best countries are the Bahamas, Cayman Islands, Cook Islands, Gibraltar and Isle of Man. In many of these it may be difficult to enforce a U.S. judgment, and in the Cook Islands it appears to be impossible.

◆ Foreign law. The trust must state that the law of the foreign jurisdiction governs interpretation of the trust.

◆ Irrevocability. The trust is irrevocable either until the grantor's death or for a set number of years. If the grantor is in financial trouble at the end of the term of years, the trust may be extended by the trustee.

◆ Anti-Duress Clause. If a court orders the grantor to attempt to obtain assets from the trust, the trustee would be compelled to refuse.

◆ Flight Clause. If there were any risk to the assets of the trust, either from a creditor or from some sort of government instability or new tax law, the trust would be transferred to another country.

- ◆ Trust Protector. An independent person, committee, or entity chosen by the grantor could have the power to change the trustee or the terms of the trust as necessary. This protector must be someone you trust absolutely. If the protector resides in the U.S., he must resign in the event of possible financial trouble of the grantor.

- ◆ Insolvency. Transfers to the trust should not be made while the grantor is insolvent, and the transfers should not make the grantor insolvent. He or she must always have other assets after the transfer.

Optional Arrangements

There are several ways of setting up an asset protection trust. Some attorneys advise putting virtually all of one's assets in such a trust while others advise only placing a small percentage. The following are some of the ways of setting up the trust.

- ◆ Liquid Assets out of the U. S. Putting cash into an offshore trust and having the trustee invest it in non-U.S. investments would offer protection both from U.S. economic problems and from seizure by creditors.

- ◆ Liquid Assets in a U. S. Brokerage Account. Using a U.S. brokerage account and having the assets titled in the offshore trust would not be as safe from creditors because assets in the U.S. may be seized by a U.S. court. But it would allow you to control them and they would not be as easy for a creditor to find as other arrangements.

- ◆ U. S. Limited Partnership Owned by a Trust. For a double layer of protection, a limited partnership can be used to hold assets (as described in Chapter 34) and the interests in the partnership can be owned by an offshore trust. This ought to stop even the most determined creditor. However, if the physical assets are in the U.S. a court which felt that you defrauded someone might decide to ignore the technical law and seize the assets anyway.

◆ U. S. Corporation Owned by a Trust. If you wish to keep personal control of your business or property, you could put it in a U.S. corporation of which you are an officer, and have the stock owned by your offshore trust.

◆ Foreign Corporation Owned by a Trust. Some countries, such as the Bahamas, allow the formation of International Business Corporations (IBCs). Such a corporation can hold your assets and be owned by your offshore trust.

◆ Real Estate Owned by Trust. Because real estate cannot be moved offshore, it is more difficult than liquid assets to protect with a trust. If a judge thinks your creditor should have it, he may allow it to be seized. However, if you have a substantial mortgage against the property the value to the creditor will be less and the cash can be put into the trust.

◆ Blind Trust Arrangement. A blind trust is one in which the beneficiary does not know what assets are owned by the trust. The benefit of this is that if a court orders you to disclose what assets are owned by the trust, you can honestly say that you do not know. You can be given general information, such as what types of securities or real estate is owned, but no specifics which would allow you to disclose the location.

◆ U.S. Co-Trustee. To insure the trust is treated as a domestic trust for tax purposes (see following section) and to maintain additional control, some prefer a trust with both a foreign trustee and a U.S. co-trustee. The problem with this is that the U.S. trustee would be subject to U.S. law. To avoid this the U.S. co-trustee should resign at the first sign of trouble.

Tax Status

As mentioned previously, a foreign asset protection trust is tax-neutral, which means it does not result in either higher or lower taxes. For tax purposes you still own the property in the offshore trust. The following is the tax status of such a trust:

◆ Income Tax. As long as you retain some power over the ultimate disposition of the trust assets, this would be considered a grantor-type trust. Under section 679 of the Internal Revenue Code (IRC), the grantor of such a trust is taxed on the income of the trust. This means the trust does not have to file its own tax returns; instead you put the income on your own return, just like with a living trust.

◆ Gift Tax. Because the grantor retains the right to change the beneficiary at death, the gift to the trust is not complete and under IRC §2511 no gift tax is owed.

◆ Estate Taxes. Assets in the trust would be considered part of the grantor's estate at death.

◆ Excise Tax. Again, because the transfer is not considered complete in a grantor-type trust, the 35% tax for transfer to a foreign entity does not apply to this type of trust. (Rev. Rul. 87-61.)

◆ Non-U.S. Trust. One matter which is not completely clear in the tax law is the effect of the classification of the trust as a U.S. or foreign trust. This determination is made based upon the following factors:

◆ where the trust was created
◆ where the trust assets are located
◆ where the trust is administered
◆ the nationality and residence of the trustee

- the nationality and residence of the person setting up the trust
- the nationality and residence of the beneficiaries of the trust

If a U.S. co-trustee is used the factors above would be about equal. However, whether the trust is U. S. or foreign the tax consequences would remain the same. The only difference is that with a foreign trust, extra tax forms would need to be filed. Because the law in uncertain in this area, some tax specialists advise that the trust be treated like a U.S. trust, but that it file the forms applicable to foreign trusts. These are:

◆ Form 926—Return of a Transferor of Property to a Foreign Corporation, Foreign Estate or Trust, or Foreign Partnership

◆ Form 1040NR—U.S. Nonresident Alien Income Tax Return

◆ Form 1041—U.S. Fiduciary Income Tax Return

◆ Form 3520A—Annual Return of a Foreign Trust with U.S. Beneficiaries

◆ Form 3520—Creation of or Transfers to Certain Foreign Trusts

When setting up your foreign trust you should rely on the opinion of an expert as to which forms to file. This will be based upon the terms of your trust.

A Possible Problem

The main problem with a foreign asset protection trust is that it is so obviously useful to defeat creditors' claims that a court could say it was set up with the "intent to defraud creditors." Intent is, of course, subjective, and you could argue that you wanted to do normal estate planning, but using such a trust looks so obviously like a way to hinder creditors that a judge might rule against you just because you have such a trust.

However, if your trust is set up right, even if the creditor wins in a U.S. court, he may be physically unable to get your offshore assets. Although some high profile criminal cases have resulted in foreign banks obeying U.S. court orders, a case based upon a civil judgment would be less likely to merit the same cooperation.

To make your offshore trust more secure, consider the following:

- ◆ If you only put a portion of your assets in the trust it would look less like you were trying to defraud creditors. (Put the rest of your assets in exempt assets at a much later time.)

- ◆ If the trust had been set up for four years when a creditor attacked it, it might be too late to attack it under the UFTA §9(b).

- ◆ If you enter into a new business or incur new debts, be sure that you have enough remaining capital so that your transfer to the trust will not be considered fraudulent.

- ◆ If you vocalize to your friends and acquaintances your fears of an economic collapse due to the national debt, your reason for setting up a foreign trust might seem more influenced by that.

- ◆ If you set up the trust many years before you have a liability you may not be required to disclose it and there may be no way it can be legally connected to you.

You should also consider that just having the trust might protect you. As explained in the chapter on limited partnerships, the years of legal work required to win such a case may scare most attorneys away, or at lease convince them to settle for less.

The Bahamas

In the Bahamas, one of the closest countries to the United States, there are hundreds of banks specializing in trusts for Americans and the government recently passed a law which makes the protections even stronger. The most important key to protection is that the trust must be set up *before* a creditor has a claim against you. Bahamian law holds that two years after the trust has been set up it cannot be touched by creditors.

You may be concerned about irrevocably turning a portion of your assets over to a stranger in a foreign country. But even though the transfer is irrevocable, you should realize that you are paying the trustee for a service like any other business, their interest is in keeping their clients happy. Just be sure to check the background and references of the company you deal with.

To set up a trust of this type you must personally visit the Bahamas and meet with an agent of the bank at least once. However, there are several "weekend excursions" and 2-day "gambling holidays" available, especially in the off-season, that offer the opportunity for a quick meeting with a trustee.

The Cook Islands

The asset protection trust laws of the Cook Islands were instigated by two lawyers from Colorado, Barry Engle and Ronald Rudman. The Cook Islands are possibly the only country in which a U.S. judgment would not be enforceable. The Cook Islands law also allows a person setting up a trust to be a beneficiary without losing the asset protection benefits.

However, the cost of this protection does not come cheap. The typical fee to set up such a trust is $15,000 to $20,000 and it can go higher.

40 Business Trusts

The business trust is one of the least understood of all legal entities. There are very few used in this country, and very few lawyers know anything about them. For this reason they can be good asset protection devices.

As an example of how limited their use is, in one large state in which nearly a hundred thousand corporations register each year, only about two dozen business trusts are formed. Because the business trust is used so infrequently, there is little information as to the legal rights of persons who deal with them. Therefore, they can serve as a successful roadblock to creditors seeking your property.

Because of the time involved in researching a new area of law, and the fact that an attorney would not want to admit to not knowing what he was doing, a creditor's attorney would probably be very willing to settle a case dealing with a business trust.

Even if he did decide to sue, every issue would probably be a new area of law which could be appealed to a higher court, dragging the case on for years and years. In the meantime, the trust could slowly wind down its business and let its assets get old.

Business trusts originated because there was a hostility in some states to corporations. For example, in some states special taxes were levied on corporations and they were forbidden from owning real estate. To gain the benefits of a corporation without these problems, lawyers devised business trusts. Because these were most prevalent in Massachusetts, they are often called "Massachusetts trusts."

Like any other type of trust, a business trust is an arrangement whereby the trustee holds property for the benefit of others. To use a business trust for asset protection purposes, you could set up your business in the form of a business trust. You could be the trustee who controls the business and the beneficiaries could be your spouse or your children. This is similar to using a corporation in the same way, but more confusing to your creditors.

A business trust can be taxed either as a trust or as a corporation. If it is a passive entity and merely holds assets for investment, it will be taxed as a trust and file IRS form 1041. If it actively runs a business then it files the corporate tax return, form 1120.

While some states require that business trusts be registered, most have no such laws. Therefore, there is no record of any of the persons in control of the business. Even where they must be registered, changes in the trustees and beneficiary may not be required.

To set up a business trust you will need to locate an attorney in your state who is willing to do some research and learn a new area of law. This may be expensive, but some attorneys may be willing to learn on their own time and only charge you for work done on your particular case. A new attorney just out of law school might be good as it would be an opportunity to be an expert in a specialized area of law and could be the basis for a book or article in a professional journal.

41 Nonprofit Corporations & Foundations

One often overlooked device for both asset protection and tax savings is the nonprofit corporation. Surely you have read the stories in the media about officers of such organizations as United Way and the Red Cross receiving salaries of hundreds of thousands of dollars. It is perfectly legal for a nonprofit corporation to pay a reasonable salary to its officers and employees.

Nonprofit Corporation

Suppose you set up an enterprise as a nonprofit corporation rather than a for-profit corporation. Your creditors could not reach the assets and you could have numerous benefits such as no sales or income tax, lower postage rates and exemption from such things as labor laws and customs duties. It is almost too good to be true.

For those in the medical profession, it is not unusual at all to have a nonprofit hospital or clinic and such an organization would not encounter much scrutiny. However, for those interested in setting up other types of businesses, the rules may require careful planning.

A nonprofit corporation is very similar to a regular corporation, except it does not have shareholders and does not distribute its profits. However, the profits can be paid to the officers and employees of the organization as salaries, as long as the amounts are reasonable.

To qualify for nontaxable status an application must be approved by the IRS. While this is a somewhat complicated form, many have been able to complete it without professional help. However, if you are setting up a corporation to protect your wealth, you may want the insurance that it is done right by hiring a professional.

Because nonprofit corporations are fairly common, it should be easy to find an attorney to set up one to suit your needs. It is possible to do it yourself. The author also wrote the book, *How to Form a Nonprofit Corporation* which is available from the publisher. The tax rules are the most complicated, so you may want to work with an accountant to get your approvals.

Foundations

For those who do not wish to set up a business, but merely to set aside part of their estate to avoid estate tax and creditors, there is the private foundation. These are primarily for wealthy individuals who plan to leave part of their estate to charity upon their deaths.

Prior to 1995 large tax deductions could be taken for donations of appreciated property, but Congress put an end to that tax loophole. Still, the foundation can be useful to wealthy individuals who wish to leave their wealth to charity.

Much information is available on setting up a foundation:

- ◆ The Council on Foundations offers publications, seminars and even free consultations with their lawyers to those contemplating setting up private foundations. Their web site is:

http://www.cof.org/

◆ The Indiana University Center on Philanthropy publishes information on setting up foundations. Their web site is:

http://www.philanthropy.iupui.edu/

◆ The Foundation Center also provides information on starting a foundation. Their web site is:

http://fdncenter.org/

Part Five - When Disaster Strikes

42 The Rules Change

Once you have a creditor, what you may and may not do with your property changes. A person who has a judgment against you is a creditor, even if you have filed an appeal. And as explained on page 29, the definition of a creditor is very broad and may even include people who have not yet filed suit. Those who have filed suit but not yet gotten a judgment can be considered creditors when it comes to determining if your transfers of property are fraudulent.

Your first impulse on learning of a claim that may result in the loss of a great amount of your property may be to sell, hide, or give away your property or to hide yourself. Depending on exactly what you do, some of these things can be legal or illegal, and others may be clearly illegal.

Keep in mind that you are not the first person who has been sued by a creditor. Millions of people over hundreds of years have been in the same situation you are in. They have already tried every trick you can think of and many more. No matter what scheme you devise to protect your assets, someone has tried it before and some court has scrutinized it. One of the leading cases in creditors' rights is from the year 1601! (*Twyne's Case*, 76 Eng. Rep. 809 (Star Chamber 1601)

As one court explained,

> Every lawyer has had the experience of being importuned at one time or another by frantic clients who wish to be stripped of their properties and have them shed in favor of spouses, relatives or friends. Such generosity is rightly suspect for largess is not the way of the world. A little friendly cross examination to plumb the depths of motive quite often brings forth the intelligence that the client has been sued, or rather, is about to be sued. He may not know it, but the law expects men to be just, before they are generous—and not the other way around. The trouble with their wish is that their intent is not really donative but rather one to thwart the oncoming creditor. Now, even the least sophisticated debtor or debtor to be, on reflection, has some hazy notion that this subterfuge won't work. More sophisticated is the approach of preferring one creditor over another, or effecting transfers to favorites where the consideration may be deemed adequate in law and doesn't involve hard cash. Of course, the *ne plus ultra* is to sell everything to innocent purchasers for value and dissipate the proceeds. Understandably, few debtors take this tack, rather, they attempt to make other "arrangements," and such arrangements are as varied and ingenious and disingenuous as people are varied, ingenious and disingenuous. *Wilkey v. Wax*, 225 N.E.2d 813 (Ill. 4 D.C.A. 1967)

In this case a man had murdered another man and was sent to prison. The wife of the decedent sued him but he had transferred all his property to his wife in a divorce settlement. The court went on to rule that people cannot use a contrived divorce settlement to avoid paying a creditor.

So, don't think that you can easily fool the system, or that no one will investigate why your net worth is suddenly zero. There are numerous records of your financial dealings and all of these can be subpoenaed.

The following chapters explore some of the options you may be considering and how useful each one may or may not be.

43 Attempting to Settle

While you may naturally not want to pay dime one to most people who make claims against you, you must realize that in most cases a small settlement payment is far better than taking a chance with our judicial system.

One of lawyers' favorite lines is "millions for defense, but not one cent for tribute." With numerous frivolous suits being filed, this may be a good practice, especially for large corporations. If you have a record of fighting and winning cases, less people will be inclined to sue you. If more people did this, there might be less unfair lawsuits filed.

However, the cost of defending even a frivolous suit is horrendous. Defending a suit for sexual harassment or discrimination could cost hundreds of thousands of dollars. Fighting a frivolous suit is a good and noble thing to do, but as a practical matter it is sometimes better to pay a small amount in tribute than five times as much to win.

In our court system even an ironclad case can be lost. A cunning lawyer, lost evidence, or a confused jury can result in a verdict which is contrary to the clear facts. Appeals are very expensive and are not available in many cases.

When you appeal a lost case, all you can appeal are the legal rulings, not the decided facts. You get only one chance to present evidence. For example, if a jury found that you called your employee a crook in front of another employee and the judge ruled it was slander, all you could appeal is whether it was legally slander. If you never said it, but the jury didn't believe you, you don't get another chance to convince another court.

When you do not have a clearly winning case there is even more reason to settle. Juries today do not seem to have a grasp of what a million dollars is and they have given away defendants' money as if it were water. Whatever settlement you are offered, consider that a jury could come in with the same amount, one-tenth that amount or ten times that amount. A party known to the author was given a chance to settle a case by paying $3,500. He refused and went to trial. He ended up owing over $30,000 including a $20,000 award and attorney fees for both sides!

If you have adopted asset protection techniques, you should be in much better position to negotiate a settlement with a claimant. If a claimant sees that you have little or no available property, he will be much more willing to settle for your insurance limits or for a smaller cash amount from you.

You usually do not have to disclose your assets to a claimant until after he has won a judgment against you. (The exceptions are if he seeks punitive damages or claims you are making fraudulent transfers.) But if your attorney provides a financial statement showing that you have few available assets, the claimant's lawyer may lose interest in pursuing the case.

Of course, you do not tell them that all your assets are in a children's trust or in your spouse's trust. If those were set up years ago they are no longer your property and do not have to be mentioned at all.

44 Bankruptcy

Bankruptcy is a procedure in which a person turns over all of his (nonexempt) property to a court and is discharged from his debts and obligations. The purpose of bankruptcy is to give a fresh start to people who have gotten over their heads in debt. Once someone reaches a point where he cannot possibly catch up on his debts, there is no use in trying.

Years ago there was a real stigma attached to filing bankruptcy and people were ashamed to use the procedure. Today, with more than a million Americans filing bankruptcy each year, most people have no qualms about it.

Whatever your feelings about it, if you are hit with an excessive judgment, bankruptcy may be your only option. Even if you hand over everything you own, your entire life's earnings may not be enough to satisfy the kind of judgments which are common today.

Some have said that bankruptcy is too easy and that people with millions of dollars in exempt assets are abusing the system. I dare say that people who are being awarded millions of dollars for such things as "emotional damages" by using psychological profiles of jurors are no less guilty of abusing the system. Your use of bankruptcy can cure the abuse of a creditor's misuse of the courts.

Bankruptcy is thousands of years old. In the Judeo-Christian Bible it states, "At the end of every seven years you shall grant a release and this is the manner of the release: every creditor shall release what he has lent to his neighbor..." Bankruptcy is also authorized by Article I of the United States Constitution, so it has noble roots. If you find it necessary to use it yourself to protect what you have spent a lifetime attaining, you should not hesitate to do so.

Stopping Creditors

One effect of filing a bankruptcy petition is that all creditors must immediately stop all actions against you. They cannot seize your property, pursue their court action, or even harass you for payment. If creditors are about to foreclose on your house or seize your car or office equipment, filing for bankruptcy can give you some breathing time.

If the creditor has a mortgage on your home or a lien on your personal property, he can usually get that property released from the bankruptcy within a short time so that he can foreclose. But the mere filing of the bankruptcy petition will stop the foreclosure and possibly give you time to catch up the payments.

Giving Security to a Creditor

Because secured creditors can get the property released from bankruptcy to foreclose on it, you should never give a creditor a lien against your exempt property. Suppose you get behind on a loan and a bank says it will sue you unless you give the bank a mortgage on your house or an assignment of your insurance policies. *Don't do it!* Those assets may be the only property you have that is exempt, and if you sign you could then lose everything you own. What you should be doing instead is selling your nonexempt property and paying down the mortgage on your home or buying more insurance. See Chapter 15.

Payments within 90 days

Any creditors you pay within 90 days of filing bankruptcy can be made to give the money back to be shared with other creditors. (Thus you cannot use all your available cash to pay that loan back to your dad and then file bankruptcy.)

Payments Within One Year

Any payments you have made or property you have transferred within a year of filing bankruptcy can be examined by the court and set aside if determined to be unfair. For example, if you sell your car to your son or give it back to the bank in a repossession, the bankruptcy trustee can bring it back into your bankruptcy estate. Even if your house has been foreclosed on the foreclosure can be set aside if the price was not fair.

Paying off debts and purchasing exempt property may cause a problem for you if you do it just before filing a bankruptcy petition, but if you have set up your affairs that way throughout your life there should be no problems.

Types of Bankruptcy

There are two types of bankruptcy for individuals, Chapter 7 and Chapter 13. If you are just temporarily behind on your debts and can catch up if given more time, Chapter 13 bankruptcy lets you reorganize your affairs and do so. If your debts are out of control, Chapter 7 bankruptcy can discharge you from your obligations. As mentioned in Chapter 4 of this book, not every debt can be discharged. Some things like taxes, child support and student loans will follow you for your entire life and then be claims against your estate when you die.

Filing for Bankruptcy

Filing for bankruptcy consists of preparing a list of those to whom you owe money, and numerous pages of details about your financial affairs. The purpose of these details is to find out if you have hidden or disposed of any property which should be turned over to your creditors.

If you must file immediately to protect your property from being seized, you don't have much flexibility. But if bankruptcy is just something you are learning about for future contingencies, it can be helpful to know what questions you will be asked, should filing bankruptcy become necessary.

To help you plan ahead, the following is information which must be provided in a bankruptcy petition:

- ◆ All names you have used in the last 6 years
- ◆ Prior bankruptcies filed in the last 6 years
- ◆ Pending bankruptcies of any spouse, partner or affiliate
- ◆ List of all real estate owned
- ◆ List of all personal property owned
- ◆ Detailed list of all current income
- ◆ Detailed list of all current expenditures
- ◆ Income from employment or business for last 2 years
- ◆ Income from other than employment or business for last 2 years
- ◆ All payments of over $600 made to creditors within 90 days of filing bankruptcy
- ◆ All payments made to creditors within 90 days of filing bankruptcy
- ◆ All suits to which you were a party within 12 months of filing bankruptcy

- ◆ All property which has been garnished or seized within 12 months of filing bankruptcy

- ◆ All property which has been repossessed, foreclosed or returned to seller within 12 months of filing bankruptcy

- ◆ All assignments made for benefit of creditors made within 120 days of filing bankruptcy

- ◆ All property which has been in the hands of a custodian, receiver or court official within one year of filing bankruptcy

- ◆ All gifts made within one year of filing bankruptcy except usual gifts to family members of under $200

- ◆ All charitable contributions of $100 or more made within one year of filing bankruptcy

- ◆ All losses to fire, theft, other casualty or gambling within one year of filing bankruptcy

- ◆ All fees paid for consultations for debt counseling within one year of filing bankruptcy

- ◆ All transfers of property other than in ordinary business within one year of filing bankruptcy

- ◆ All financial accounts closed or transferred to another person within one year of filing bankruptcy

- ◆ All safe deposit boxes in which you had any valuables within one year of filing bankruptcy

- ◆ All setoffs made by any creditor within 90 days of filing bankruptcy

- ◆ All payments made to creditors who were insiders within 12 months of filing bankruptcy

- ◆ All suits and administrative proceedings against you within the last year

- ◆ All repossessions and foreclosures against you within the last year

- ◆ All gifts you made within the last year
- ◆ All fire, theft, casualty and gambling losses within the last year
- ◆ All financial accounts and safe deposit boxes closed within the last year
- ◆ All property which other persons are holding for you
- ◆ All addresses used by you in the last 2 years
- ◆ All businesses in which you were involved in the last two years
- ◆ All bookkeepers and accountants you have used in the last 6 years
- ◆ All persons or firms which have audited your books or prepared your financial statements within the last 2 years
- ◆ All persons who are in possession of your books of account and records
- ◆ All financial institutions to whom you have given a financial statement within the last two years
- ◆ The last 2 inventories of your property and who took them
- ◆ All withdrawals of funds from your business in the last year

As you can see, any gifts to family, gambling losses, or other transfers of property will be closely scrutinized. However, if it happened several years before filing for bankruptcy, the issue might not even come up.

Knowing that some debts may not be discharged and that some assets may be kept after bankruptcy, you can arrange your affairs so that you always pay your nondischargeable debts first and that the only property you own is property which is exempt from creditors. (The bankruptcy system is meant to examine your affairs after you have gotten into trouble. Some may say you have an unfair advantage in learning these rules far in advance.)

Denial of Discharge

The purpose of bankruptcy is for a court to discharge a debtor from his debts. After this has been done, the debtor can safely own property and former creditors (whose debts were wiped out) can do nothing. Under section 727(a) of the Bankruptcy Act a debtor's discharge is automatic unless one or more of the following circumstances is present:

- ◆ The debtor made a fraudulent conveyance within a year of filing bankruptcy.
- ◆ The debtor has no financial records.
- ◆ The debtor made a false oath, false claim, paid someone to affect the outcome, or withheld records.
- ◆ The debtor lied about his or her assets.
- ◆ The debtor failed to testify after being given immunity.
- ◆ The debtor did any of the above in a related bankruptcy case.
- ◆ The debtor has been discharged within the last six years.
- ◆ The debtor waived the right to discharge in writing.
- ◆ The debtor is not an individual.

As you can see, you cannot destroy your records or take the Fifth Amendment to try to protect your assets. But by planning early, you can be sure your affairs are arranged so that you can go through bankruptcy honestly and painlessly and not do any of these things.

One thing to consider is that there is a big difference between a court saying a transfer was fraudulent and denying a discharge. If a court rules that something you did was fraudulent it can undo it, or even put you in jail. If the court merely denies your discharge, you may be able to keep all your exempt property. You will just be in the situation that your creditors will not go away. You will have to avoid holding any nonexempt property in your name.

Bankruptcy Reform

For the last several years several business groups, notably credit card companies have been trying to get Congress to revise the bankruptcy laws to make it more difficult for people to wipe out their debts (especially credit card debts).

It looked like the recent reform bill would become law and President Bush was expected to sign it. (MBNA, one of the biggest credit card companies was a big Republican contributor in 2000.) But because the bill contained a provision that abortion protestors couldn't discharge judgments against them in bankruptcy, it died.

Of course the bill will come up again, so watch for it in the news. One of the worst proposals is to forbid states from allowing unlimited homestead exemptions. Various proposals were to lower it to $125,000 or $250,000 and to require a debtor to live there for two or four years before being allowed the exemption. The latest information is that President Bush would veto a bill that limits the homestead exemption. (Texas has an unlimited exemption.)

If the bankruptcy reform bill ever passes, Galt Press will provide a free summary of the law to all purchasers of this book. Just e-mail us at: bankruptcyupdate@galtpress.com or send your mailing address to Galt Press, P O Box 8, Clearwater, FL 33757.

45 Hiding Your Assets

People commonly try to protect assets from creditors by simply hiding them. However, this method can be both illegal and unsuccessful.

Everyone is free to hide his or her assets anywhere they deem safe. This can mean burying them in the yard or storing them in the basement at mother's house. Nothing is illegal about that. The problem arises when a person must answer questions at a deposition or file a bankruptcy petition. If you own an asset but have hidden it or given it to someone else to hold and you lie under oath, you have committed perjury, which is a crime. If you are caught you may go to jail.

And you can't usually get by with tricky answers. If you try to evade an answer a good lawyer will continue asking questions to get to the truth. You will be asked what happened to property you owned and what happened to the proceeds if you sold it. You will be asked if any of your property is in the possession of another person. You are legally required to answer truthfully under oath.

If your entire financial future is at stake and you feel that a judgment against you is unjust or the system is corrupt, you may feel that it is your moral right to protect what you have earned by lying, even under oath. If you decide to ignore the legal system you must realize what the potential consequences are and what you are up against.

There are many ways of discovering your assets. Your tax returns may be subpoenaed from the IRS. If you think you can keep a bank account or a piece of property secret, you will probably be given away by your tax return. If you listed interest or deductions or depreciation on your tax return, the property will be discovered.

Most people do not realize the sophisticated ways assets or income can be found. For example, you may think there is no way for anyone to find out about cash received in your business. However, if an audit were made of the number of products you purchased and compared to the number you claimed to have used, a discrepancy would indicate unreported income. For example, the IRS once used the number of napkins a restaurant had laundered to prove how many dinners they served!

Gold, jewelry, gems and other collectibles do not show up on your tax return, and often these can be easily hidden. During World War II some people who left Nazi areas first bought rare stamps and stuck them on family letters which were not even checked at customs. But there are ways these things can be discovered. A creditor can subpoena your checking account and charge card records. If you bought your collectibles by check or credit card there is a permanent record. If you insured them there is probably a cancelled check for the insurance. If you kept them in a safe deposit box there is probably a cancelled check for the box rental.

Some people erroneously believe that the Fifth Amendment to the Constitution protects them from being required to disclose their assets. But this right only applies to criminal matters. In a civil suit you cannot use the Fifth Amendment to protect yourself.

If you plan to protect your assets by hiding them you must be aware of all the ways they can be found and what the penalties are if you are convicted of lying under oath.

Further Research

Roark, Dominique, "Should You Lie Under Oath?" Galt Press

46 Hiding Yourself

One reaction some people have to the threat of litigation is to run and hide. This is not a criminal offense, but it may not be a successful way to avoid liability, either.

The Legal Side

Under the legal principle of due process a person cannot be made subject to a court order unless he has been notified of the pending action and given a chance to respond. Originally this meant that the papers had to be personally handed to him by a sheriff. This is called service of process.

However, as transportation and communication have improved, states have passed laws making it easier to subject people to lawsuits. Because people travel so often across state lines by automobile, all states have laws which allow victims of auto accidents to sue nonresidents where the accident took place and to serve them easily.

The laws say that anyone who makes use of a state's roads automatically consents to "constructive" service of process. This service against nonresidents or residents who conceal themselves can be made by sending one copy of the court papers to the secretary of state and a copy by mail to the defendant.

The same principle used for automobile drivers also applies to those who do business in the state and to other categories of persons as listed in each state's laws. Therefore, if you have conducted a business such as a medical or dental practice in a state, you cannot avoid liability by closing up shop and hiding. In fact, hiding may hurt you. Former patients with claims against you could file suits and serve you by constructive service and then place judgment liens on any property of yours they can locate. In this case, even if you had a good defense to the suit you could not present it because you would be unaware of the suit. Once a judgment is rendered and a creditor has tracked you down to seize your assets, it is often too late to assert your defense.

If you remain in the state and just hide from the process server, that usually won't help you. If the sheriff finds you at home, but you do not open the door, the papers can be left on your doorstep or they can be read to you through the door.

Also, if you move to another state you can be served by a sheriff in that state. If the lawyer knows your address he can have the summons mailed to the sheriff in the county in which you live, and have it served upon you there. The fact that you are hundreds or thousands of miles from the trial makes it a lot more difficult for you to defend yourself and you may be required to return for depositions and for trial.

The Practical Side

While a plaintiff could pursue you if you were not locatable, as a practical matter your absence would make it a lot less likely that a case would be pursued, especially if you did not leave property behind. Lawyers like easy cases. They don't like cases that will take years to fight with unsure results. Therefore, if you do conceal yourself it may help you avoid suits. This is especially true if you have been private about your wealth (see the next chapter).

Not all lawyers are familiar with suing missing persons and some may not even want to take on such a case. Unless your claimant can find a specialist you may be safe.

If you are nearing retirement, and have always wanted to move to somewhere like Florida, Arizona, or Montana, doing so without leaving forwarding addresses may help you avoid litigation. You don't have to be secretive about it and disappear. You could buy a motor home or a houseboat and tell everyone you are going to travel around for a few years.

If you choose this option, be sure you cannot be located. Once you have been served with court papers, you must obey every order from the court. Even if you don't receive the orders you have the responsibility to find out what they are.

Don't tell anyone your new address and don't put in a change of address order with the post office. (Anyone can get your new address from the post office.)

Obviously, moving without leaving an address will take some planning. You will need to start months ahead of time closing accounts and opening new ones. For your new accounts you should use a post office box.

If you have a dear and trusted friend in another city you could get a post office box there and ask him or her to forward your mail every month. Or, if you will be moving to somewhere near a state line, you could rent a box across the line. This way, if creditors tried to trace you in that state's records (driver license, tax records, etc.) you would not be listed.

If you are travelling around the country you could have your mail sent to a motel by overnight courier once a month.

After you have moved away you might want to return to your former home in order to attend weddings, funerals or other important events. Before you do, you should check to see if any suits have been filed against you. Lawyers have been known to use such events to catch people they are looking for. By calling the state and federal courts in the area you can find out if any lawsuits have been filed in your absence. Usually the clerk can also tell you where the case stands. For example, if the clerk says "waiting for return of service" you know someone is trying to find you to serve the papers on you.

Even if no case has yet been filed, you still might get caught if you return. A lawyer who didn't want to file a case while you were away might file it the morning of your arrival and serve you the same day.

Divorce, Alimony and Child Support

The rules explained previously for constructive service of process only apply to certain types of cases such as using an automobile in a state and doing business in the state. They do not apply to other cases, such as divorce and child support actions. For these kinds of cases the plaintiff has to actually find you and serve the papers on you in order to get a money judgment.

A court can grant a divorce against you in your absence by publishing a notice in the newspaper, but it may not deal in financial matters without personal service. If you are ever found, however, you can be held liable for alimony and/or child support for the years you were missing. Therefore, if you plan to disappear it must be permanent.

If you have already been served with divorce papers, disappearing won't help you. Once you are a party to a case you are responsible for providing a current address and orders can be entered against you in your absence and without your knowledge. Failure to obey could result in your arrest.

Leaving the Country

A surprising number of Americans, scared by litigation, crime and the national deficit, and tired of high taxes and government over-regulation, are moving abroad. While no Americans gave up their citizenship in 1982, hundreds did each year in the 1990s. A Ford Motor Company director, a Campbell's Soup Co. heir, and the founder of Carnival Cruise Lines, all have left in recent years.

Merely leaving the U.S. will not lower your taxes, however. The United States is one of the few countries which significantly taxes the worldwide income of citizens overseas. To avoid U.S. income and estate taxes you would have to renounce your citizenship. Even then, if it suspects that your reason for leaving is to save on taxes, the U.S. government demands you continue to pay taxes for ten years after you leave! Of course, finding you assessing the tax and collecting it once you are gone would be difficult. But if you plan to return periodically you would have problems.

Once your U.S. income tax liability ceases you may be free of income tax forever. Several countries have no income or estate taxes whatsoever, saving millions for those who take up residency there.

If moving out of state sounds like a big decision, becoming an expatriate is immeasurably bigger. For both patriotic, practical and emotional reasons, Americans agonize over the decision. Many cannot do it. We have known this is the greatest country in the world from earliest childhood.

Before renouncing your citizenship you need to find a new country which will have you. Ireland and Israel grant citizenship quickly based on ancestry. Canada will grant citizenship after three years. St. Kitts-Nevis in the Caribbean requires the purchase of $150,000 in real estate and a $50,000 fee. However, before deciding on a new country you should investigate its tax system and other restrictions on freedom. After a few months there you may find life to be less desirable than you imagined.

If you do renounce your citizenship you will be limited in your ability to visit the U.S. The first year you can only stay

30 days. In future years you can stay 100 to 120 days. However, with computers, fax machines, cable TVs and cellular phones the U.S. may not seem as far as you actually are.

Less drastic than renouncing your citizenship is merely moving abroad. While this will not affect your taxes it may protect you from lawsuits. Many Americans have retired to such places as Costa Rica, Mexico and Poland where their social security check goes farther.

Your biggest concern if moving abroad should be the value of the dollar. While it is strong now, there is a very real risk of devaluation in the future. If you plan to live only on social security, your monthly check may slowly become worthless in the local currency. If you have other assets you should place some of them into hard assets and diversify the rest among a few different currencies.

If you leave the country just to avoid lawsuits, you still should keep your exact whereabouts a secret. It is possible to serve a summons on a person in another country. If you are served personally in another country a personal judgment can be entered against you.

References:

Bauman, Robert E., *The Complete Guide to Offshore Residency, Dual Citizenship and Second Passports*

Beaver, William, *Overseas Americans: The Essential Guide To Living And Working Abroad*

Carter, Jimmy, *U. S. Law Affecting Americans Living and Working Abroad*

Hess, Melissa Brayer and Linderman, Patricia, *The Expert Expatriate: Your Guide to Successful Relocation Abroad: Moving, Living, Thriving*

Starchild, Adam, *How to Legally Obtain a Second Citizenship and Passport-And Why You Want to*

47 Enjoying Your Assets

If you find yourself in a situation where you know you will be liable for a large claim, and you know you cannot legally shift or give away your assets, you have another alternative. You can spend your money on yourself.

Perhaps you have been frugal all your life. You rarely went to nice restaurants, always bought a used car, clipped coupons to save a few dollars here and there. Now someone wants a million dollars from you because they tripped over their own feet on your property?

There is no law forbidding you from spending your own money on yourself. You cannot give it away, or sell it for less than it is worth. You can't even burn your money, you can be forced to pay it back out of future earnings. But you can enjoy your money. Perhaps its time to start going to good restaurants, buying a new car, taking a trip you have always wanted? You can't give your grandkids thousands of dollars each after you have a large claim, but you can take them on the vacation of their lifetime.

Lawsuits can take a long time. If they are appealed and reversed and retried, they can last many years. If you buy a new Jaguar today, you will at least have a year or two of enjoyment out of it. If you know you will lose, you might even prefer to spend your money on your lawyer than to give it to your creditor.

There are rules that you cannot borrow money just before filing bankruptcy, and then discharge the debt. But if you have the cash, you have the right to spend it on yourself. You can sell property you own at a fair price and spend the money on things you have always wanted.

But like anything else in law, you cannot look like a hog. You cannot be too greedy or too obvious. If you merely improve your standard of living, you should be able to get away with it.

Keep in mind that while personal property like a boat or jewelry can be taken by a creditor, things like cruises, ski trips, operas, ballets, manicures, exotic spas, massages, and great dinners cannot be taken away. Buy a hundred pizzas for the foster children in your town.

If you are brought before a judge in bankruptcy court and accused of wasting your assets, be humble. Don't say you'd rather burn the money than see the creditor get it. Explain to the judge how hard you've worked all your life, talk about the money you gave to charity. Tell him how many years you didn't take a vacation, and how fixed your old car rather than splurge on a new one. Explain that you only have a limited number of years left and that you thought your wife deserved to see Europe with you just once. If you have a medical condition, be sure to mention it!

Part Six - Your Immediate Action Plan

48 Evaluate Your Exposure

The first thing to do in setting up your asset protection plan is to evaluate who your potential creditors are and which property you own can be seized by them.

First sit down with your financial statement and the list of your state's exemptions in Appendix B of this book and determine what property might be exposed and what is exempt from creditors' claims.

Next, go through Chapter 2 and note which risks you might face in the coming years. Do you own a boat? Do you have a teenager who drives? Are you in a partnership with other professionals? Do you own rental properties in your own name?

Do you have liabilities which cannot be protected against by exempting your assets? Remember that such things as environmental claims, taxes, alimony and child support can never be discharged. They can even be claims against exempt property and claims against your estate after you die. The only way to protect against them is to have no property in your name.

How much insurance do you have? Do you have an umbrella policy? What would it cost to increase it to $2 million? $5 million? Is your professional insurance enough to cover you for a serious loss?

Make lists of your risks, your insurance, your assets and assets you expect to acquire in the future both through your earnings and inheritance.

Have an insolvency analysis done on your situation. This will determine, under your state's laws, how much property you can shield and still be considered solvent.

If you live in one of the states with favorable exemptions you may be in good shape and not need to make many changes. In other states you may find yourself totally exposed. Possibly everything you own could be lost if a lawsuit were filed against you tomorrow.

If your main risks are those which can be protected against with exempt assets your next step is to find out more details on your state's exemptions from a specialist as discussed in the next chapter.

If you are more concerned about liabilities such as alimony, taxes and environmental claims you will need an offshore trust as described in Chapter 39.

49 Get an Exemption Analysis

If you have invested in this book, you have or expect to have assets worth protecting. To be sure to protect those assets, you need to have accurate, up-to-date information on the laws of your state and the best place to get that information is from an attorney who specializes in that area of law.

I know, you hate to go to attorneys. They overcharge, they're arrogant and they're condescending. People don't like to go to doctors or dentists either, but these are some of the unfortunate necessities of life.

Begin by finding a good attorney who specializes in bankruptcy and ask for a consultation. Some bankruptcy attorneys give free consultations, but those are intended for people who are actually contemplating bankruptcy and are for the purpose of signing up the client. Because you want valuable information from the attorney, you should expect to pay for the attorney's time. You will need half an hour or an hour and should expect to pay $100 or $200 per hour.

The purpose of your consultation is to find out exactly what assets are exempt from creditors in your state at the time. Appendix B of this manual includes a State Exemption Worksheet to use in talking with the attorney. You should use this form to obtain the detailed information you will need to protect your assets.

One possible way to protect yourself further and have more accurate information would be to ask the attorney for an opinion letter listing exactly what the exemptions are. A legal opinion put on paper will be more thoroughly researched than one given to you orally at a consultation. If he puts his opinion on paper and you rely on it and lose your property, you may be able to sue him if you get erroneous advice and lose some property you expected to keep. However, he will probably charge a couple hundred dollars for such a letter. If he is smart he will probably put a lot of caveats in the letter that it can't be sure a court will rule the way his analysis expects. Also, the fact that you obtained such a letter might be used against you to prove you were planning to defraud some creditors.

One thing you should realize is that law is more like an art than a science. There are often no exact answers. In one case a trial court ruled one way but was reversed by the appellate court. Then the state supreme court looked at the case and reversed the appellate court. Was that the final answer? No, the losing party appealed to the United States Supreme Court and they reversed the state supreme court.

Now, if a state supreme court does not know what the law is, how can you expect a mere lawyer to know? You can't. Therefore, you should get a second, or even a third opinion. If you are protecting a half-million or a million dollar estate, surely it is worth two or three $100 consultations to get the best advice on how to best protect your estate.

When meeting with your lawyer you must realize that the process of going to law school is what made him or her so arrogant. Law students are among the brightest out of college, but in their first days of law school they are made to feel incompetent and inadequate in the face of the body of law with which they are presented.

The new law student is given a series of judges' opinions to read which may consist of a 1957 New York case followed by an 1830 English case and then a 1983 California case. The cases use legal terms never before seen by the student. The logic is sometimes excellent and sometimes flawed, and the student is not told which is which. Soon the student realizes how inadequate he is compared to the professors, judges and lawyers who appear godlike. But three years later when he graduates, he figures he has reached the exalted state which had previously held him in awe, and is amazed at his own intellectual abilities.

Keep this in mind when meeting with your lawyer. The fact that you are attempting to understand the legal system and take action to use it to your benefit may intimidate your lawyer. He or she would prefer that you throw yourself at his or her mercy and just ask for advice. He or she may denigrate a manual like this which can help a layman understand the law. Act impressed but get the information you are paying for.

Legal Research

If you absolutely refuse to go to an attorney for an exemption analysis, you can do some research yourself. However, the answers will not be easy to find. You need to find all the statutes, and then read all the court cases that interpret the statutes. Sometimes the statutes say something that seems clear, but when you read the court cases you realize it means something else completely.

To start you need a list of the bankruptcy exemptions in your state. You can get this from a book on filing for bankruptcy, or from a web site which provides bankruptcy advice.

A good book with the information is *How to File Your Own Bankruptcy (or How to Avoid It)* by Edward A. Haman. It is available in most bookstores and libraries. Another is *How to File for Chapter 7 Bankruptcy* by Stephen Elias. These list every exemption for each state and then list the statute citations. You can look up the statutes to get the exact wording of the law.

You can also find the bankruptcy exemptions on several sites on the Internet. These may be more up to date than the books, but they might not be as reliable since you never know who prepared them. A few the author found as this book went to press are:

http://www.thebankruptcysite.com/what_do_i_keep.htm

http://www.filing-bankruptcy-form.com/list-of-exemptions.html

http://joehager.com/bankruptcy/pdfexemptiontables/states.htm

You can find others by putting "state bankruptcy exemptions" in a search engine such as www.google.com.

Once you have the statute citations you should check an "annotated" version of the statutes. This is a copy that has a summary of each applicable court case listed under each statute. When you find cases that relate to your situation you can then look up the entire case opinion to get the facts.

You should check a book on legal research to be sure you understand what you are doing. Some states have more than one bankruptcy court and it is possible that the bankruptcy court in your district does not follow a ruling made by the bankruptcy case in another district in your state. (This is why getting the opinion of an attorney in your area would be more accurate.)

50 Set Up Your Plan

If you have read through this book to this point you have a good understanding of how to protect yourself from claims, what property is safe from creditors and how to protect the rest of what you own. If you want to be sure not to lose what you have worked so hard for, you should start immediately arranging your affairs to protect what you own.

Throughout this manual the same message keeps coming up: If the planning had taken place sooner the asset would be safe. Once a problem arises it is too late to take most steps which would be effective.

After you have analyzed your exposure (Chapter 48) and conferred with an attorney (Chapter 49) you can sit down and plan your strategy. Compare the equity in your home with your state's exemption. Should you pay off your mortgage or get a bigger mortgage?

If pension plans or IRAs are exempt in your state, have you invested as much as you possibly can in one? Should you set up another type of plan which would allow you to put away more money?

If annuities are protected in your state, have you sold your nonexempt assets and put the proceeds into an annuity? Have you considered an offshore annuity? This may protect you even if annuities are not exempt in your state.

If you are in business, have you formed a corporation or limited liability company? Have you considered setting up several such entities to divide your assets and your risks?

In planning your asset protection strategy, you have several levels of protection to choose from. These range from the most basic level in which you can merely avoid risk and invest in protected assets, to the most advanced level, in which you set up several legal devices including several entities and an offshore trust.

Basic Asset Protection   Cost: Under $500

If you don't want to put a great deal of effort into protecting your estate, but are still concerned about your potential losses, you can do four things which will give you basic protection:

Avoid risk. In your professional life avoid cases and situations which involve higher risk. Don't volunteer for or participate in anything which could result in liability. Don't buy risky investments like real estate without a careful contract and a corporate shield against liability.

Buy insurance. Don't settle for 100/300 limits on your liability policies. You should have at least $1 million in coverage, preferably more. If you are in a risky profession, look into higher limits on your professional liability coverage.

Know and use your exemptions. Contribute as much as possible to a qualified pension plan. Check the exemptions in Appendix A for your state and keep them in mind when buying assets.

Keep your finances private. You may not ever want to lie under oath, but by keeping your wealth private you will be less likely to be a target for lawsuits. Don't fill out any survey or product registration that asks for your personal information.

Intermediate Asset Protection   Cost: $500 to $2,000

If you are willing to take some immediate action to protect your assets, but do not want to spend a lot of time or money, you can do some basic things which will provide protection far beyond their expense. Besides doing everything in the previous section, you should:

Incorporate. Any business you are involved in should either be a corporation or limited liability company. Be sure that you follow the formalities for corporations and keep your minutes up to date.

Form an LLC. While a corporation (or LLC) is a good shield against business risks, as explained in chapter 32 in most states a limited liability company will protect your assets from creditors. Put your vulnerable assets in an LLC.

Use land trusts. If your state allows land trusts, be sure that all investment real estate you own is owned by land trusts.

Obtain contracts. Have a lawyer prepare contracts for your employees and clients or patients. Make the use of them routine. Don't deal with anyone who refuses to sign one. Use protective contracts in every venture which involves risk.

Shift assets. Have an attorney who specializes in bankruptcy law prepare a list for you of what assets are exempt in your state. Ask him to review the most recent cases of people who converted nonexempt assets into exempt assets. Find out what is allowed and what is forbidden.

Advanced Asset Protection   Cost: $2,000 to $5,000

If you wish to take additional steps to protect your assets you should consult with an attorney who will be able to set up trusts and partnerships which give stronger protections than simpler arrangements.

Set up several LLCs. By setting up several limited liability companies you can divide your risks even further. In some states LLC filing fees are as cheap as $10 or $15 a year.

Irrevocable trusts. Depending upon whom you wish your assets to eventually go to, you can set up trusts for your spouse, your children or a charity.

Limited partnerships. A limited partnership can protect your property from both creditors and spousal claims in the event of divorce. For extra protection you should set up two or more partnerships and divide your assets among them.

Nonprofit corporation or foundation. If you can convert all or part of your business into a nonprofit corporation, you can both protect it from creditors and pay less taxes. If you intend to give to charity you can set up a foundation.

Domestic asset protection trusts. Alaska, Delaware, Nevada and Rhode Island offer domestic asset protection trusts.

Offshore LLCs. All of the benefits of a regular LLC are enhanced by setting one up offshore.

Maximum Asset Protection   Cost: $15,000 to $20,000

If you have a large estate and want to do whatever it takes to protect it, you will need to make arrangements outside the country to put the highest available protection around your property.

Offshore trusts. The Bahamas, Cayman Islands, Cook Islands, Isle of Man, Gibraltar, and Turks and Caicos have trust companies which offer asset protection trusts. You can deal directly, but are well advised to be represented by an American attorney who can protect your interests.

Common risks and possible protections

Risk	Don't sign a guaranty	Corporation	Insurance	Contracts	Exempt property	Ltd. Partnership Lim. Liab. Co.	Offshore Trusts	Gifts
Bills (Medical, legal business, etc.)	●	●	●	●	●	●	●	●
Loans	●	●		●	●	●	●	●
Child Support						●	●	●
Malpractice			●	●	●	●	●	●
Accidents		●	●		●	●	●	●
Acts of others		●	●	●	●	●	●	●
Torts (Battery, slander)					●	●	●	●
Labor/Civil Rights violations		●			●	●	●	●
Alimony				●	●	●	●	●
Environmental violations		●				●	●	●
Taxes				●		●	●	●

How Asset Protection Works

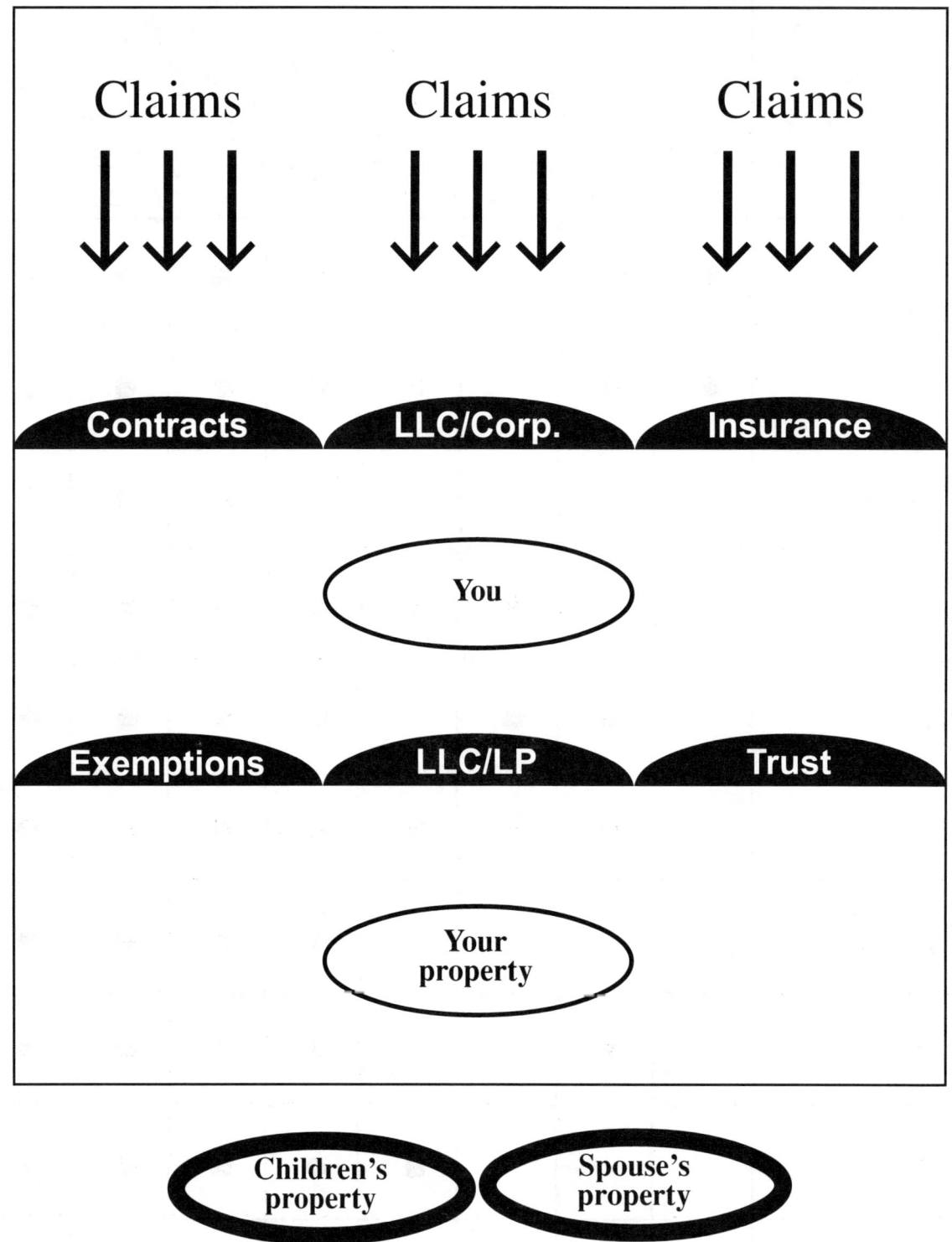

The claims against you are first deflected by contracts, entities such as LLCs and corporations and insurance. Any claims that get through your first line of defence and reach you, can't get your property which is protected by exemptions, limited liability companies, limited partmnerships and trusts. Other property which is in the name of your spouse and children is not even in the picture.

51 A Final Word

One unfortunate aspect of American law is that in many situations there are no black and white answers. In some cases converting assets may have been allowed while in other cases which appear identical, the same actions may have been disallowed. In some cases people who put all their property into a friend's name the night before a deposition get off scott free because the lawyers don't ask the right questions, and in other cases people who make elaborate asset protection plans lose their property because the judge looks carefully at everything and finds a flaw.

It is with this uncertainty that you must create your asset protection program. The reason for this is that our legal system gives judges flexibility to do what they think is fair under the circumstances.

Even the most experienced attorney can be wrong. Trial judges are overruled by appellate judges, and appellate judges are overruled by state supreme court judges. State supreme court judges are overruled by the U. S. Supreme Court. How can you expect your local attorney to know how the law will be interpreted? You can't.

Therefore, you should never "put all of your eggs in one basket." You should diversify your assets and use several of the asset protection techniques found in this manual.

If you do end up in court, you must under all circumstances look like the "good guy." If you look like you are hiding something or are not telling the truth or are trying to trick the court, the law will be interpreted against you.

When appearing in court you must at all times be respectful, even reverent. If you are arrogant and display an attitude of disrespect for the judge or the system, then you will be more likely to lose your case. But if you appear honest and forthright and seem to be doing everything to comply with the law, the judge may have some sympathy for your plight and interpret the law in your favor.

Also keep in mind that for every case that turned out poorly for the debtor, there were hundreds of cases which didn't even get to court. Only a small percentage of people ever have million dollar claims against them, and only a percentage of claimants seek more than the insurance available. Of those, few have attorneys who are willing to contest each type of asset protection device. So if you have set up several devices to protect your estate, each one will make it less likely that someone will pursue the case further and get to all of your assets.

You can protect that for which you have worked your whole life. If you take control and use the laws that are available to you, you will be way ahead of those who let life happen to them. The information is in this book. It is up to you to use it.

I wish you the best.

A State Exemption Summaries

This appendix contains a summary of the most important exemptions in each state. Use this to get a rough idea what are the best protections in your state. Keep in mind that these are just summaries. The actual exemptions may be higher or lower depending on other factors such as if you are married or disabled or are a farmer. Personal property may be limited to a dollar amount or to specific items such as clothing and a Bible. See chapter 49 for information on how to get more details on your state's exemptions.

Alabama
Homestead	$5,000
Vehicle	-
Annuity/Ins.	Yes
Pensions	Yes
Personal prop.	$3,000
Tools	Military
Business partn.	No

Alaska
Homestead	$64,800
Vehicle	$3,600
Annuity/Ins.	Yes
Pensions	Yes
Personal prop.	$3,600
Tools	$3,360
Business partn.	Yes

Arizona
Homestead	$100,000
Vehicle	$5,000
Annuity/Ins.	Yes
Pensions	Yes
Personal prop.	$200+
Tools	$2,500
Business partn.	No

Arkansas
Homestead	Unlimited
Vehicle	$1,200
Annuity/Ins.	Yes
Pensions	Yes
Personal prop.	$500+
Tools	$750
Business partn.	Yes

California – System 1
Homestead	$50,000
Vehicle	$1,900
Annuity/Ins.	Yes
Pensions	Yes
Personal prop.	$5,000+
Tools	$5,000
Business partn.	Yes

California – System 2
Homestead	$17,425
Vehicle	$2,725
Annuity/Ins.	Yes
Pensions	Yes
Personal prop.	$925+
Tools	$1,750
Business partn.	No

Colorado
Homestead	$45,000
Vehicle	$3,000
Annuity/Ins.	Yes
Pensions	Yes
Personal prop.	$3,000+
Tools	$25,000
Business partn.	Yes

Connecticut
Homestead	$75,000
Vehicle	$1,500
Annuity/Ins.	Yes
Pensions	Yes
Personal prop.	$1,000+
Tools	Yes
Business partn.	No

Delaware
Homestead	None
Vehicle	-
Annuity/Ins.	Yes
Pensions	Yes
Personal prop.	$500+
Tools	$75
Business partn.	Yes

District of Columbia
Homestead	Any
Vehicle	$2,575
Annuity/Ins.	Yes
Pensions	Yes
Personal prop.	$8,625+
Tools	$1,625
Business partn.	No

Florida
Homestead	Unlimited
Vehicle	$1,000
Annuity/Ins.	Yes
Pensions	Yes
Personal prop.	$1,000+
Tools	No
Business partn.	No

Georgia
Homestead	$10,000
Vehicle	$3,500
Annuity/Ins.	Yes
Pensions	Yes
Personal prop.	$5,000+
Tools	$1,500
Business partn.	No

Hawaii
Homestead	$20,000
Vehicle	$2,575
Annuity/Ins.	Yes
Pensions	Yes
Personal prop.	$1,000+
Tools	Yes
Business partn.	Yes

Idaho
Homestead	$50,000
Vehicle	$3,000
Annuity/Ins.	Yes
Pensions	Yes
Personal prop.	$5,000+
Tools	Yes
Business partn.	Yes

Illinois
Homestead	$7,500
Vehicle	$1,200
Annuity/Ins.	Yes
Pensions	Yes
Personal prop.	$2,000
Tools	$750
Business partn.	Yes

Indiana
Homestead	$7,500
Vehicle	-
Annuity/Ins.	Yes
Pensions	Yes
Personal prop.	$4,000+
Tools	Yes
Business partn.	Yes

Iowa
Homestead	Unlimited
Vehicle	See pers.prop.
Annuity/Ins.	Yes
Pensions	Yes
Personal prop.	$5,000+
Tools	$10,000
Business partn.	No

Kansas
Homestead	Unlimited
Vehicle	$20,000
Annuity/Ins.	Yes
Pensions	Yes
Personal prop.	$1,000+
Tools	$7,500
Business partn.	No

Kentucky
Homestead	$5,000
Vehicle	$2,500
Annuity/Ins.	Yes
Pensions	Yes
Personal prop.	$3,000+
Tools	Yes
Business partn.	Yes

Louisiana
Homestead	$25,000
Vehicle	-
Annuity/Ins.	Yes
Pensions	Yes
Personal prop.	$5,000+
Tools	Yes
Business partn.	No

Maine
Homestead	$25,000
Vehicle	$5,000
Annuity/Ins.	Yes
Pensions	Yes
Personal prop.	$6,000+
Tools	$5,000+
Business partn.	Yes

Maryland
Homestead	None
Vehicle	-
Annuity/Ins.	Yes
Pensions	Yes
Personal prop.	$5,500+
Tools	$2,500
Business partn.	Yes

Massachusetts
Homestead	$300,000
Vehicle	$700
Annuity/Ins.	Yes
Pensions	Yes
Personal prop.	$3,000+
Tools	$500
Business partn.	Yes

Michigan
Homestead	$3,500
Vehicle	-
Annuity/Ins.	Yes
Pensions	Yes
Personal prop.	$1,000+
Tools	$1,000
Business partn.	Yes

Minnesota
Homestead	$200,000
Vehicle	$3,600
Annuity/Ins.	Yes
Pensions	Yes
Personal prop.	$8,100
Tools	$13,000
Business partn.	Yes

Mississippi
Homestead	$75,000
Vehicle	Yes
Annuity/Ins.	Yes
Pensions	Yes
Personal prop.	$10,000
Tools	See pers. prop.
Business partn.	Yes

Missouri
Homestead	$8,000
Vehicle	$1,000
Annuity/Ins.	Yes
Pensions	Yes
Personal prop.	$1,000+
Tools	$2,000
Business partn.	Yes

Montana
Homestead	$60,000
Vehicle	$2,500
Annuity/Ins.	Yes
Pensions	Yes
Personal prop.	$4,500+
Tools	$3,000
Business partn.	No

Nebraska
Homestead	$12,500
Vehicle	-
Annuity/Ins.	Yes
Pensions	Yes
Personal prop.	$1,500+
Tools	$2,400
Business partn.	Yes

Nevada
Homestead	$125,000
Vehicle	$4,500
Annuity/Ins.	Yes
Pensions	Yes
Personal prop.	$3,000+
Tools	$4,500
Business partn.	Yes

New Hampshire
Homestead	$30,000
Vehicle	$4,000
Annuity/Ins.	Yes
Pensions	Yes
Personal prop.	$3,500+
Tools	$5,000
Business partn.	Yes

New Jersey
Homestead	None
Vehicle	-
Annuity/Ins.	Yes
Pensions	Yes
Personal prop.	$1,000+
Tools	No
Business partn.	No

New Mexico
Homestead	$30,000
Vehicle	$4,000
Annuity/Ins.	Yes
Pensions	Yes
Personal prop.	$2,500+
Tools	$1,500
Business partn.	Yes

New York
Homestead	$10,000
Vehicle	$2,400
Annuity/Ins.	Yes
Pensions	Yes
Personal prop.	$5,000
Tools	$600
Business partn.	Yes

North Carolina
Homestead	$10,000
Vehicle	$1,500
Annuity/Ins.	Yes
Pensions	Yes
Personal prop.	$3,500+
Tools	$750
Business partn.	Yes

North Dakota
Homestead	$80,000
Vehicle	$1,200
Annuity/Ins.	Yes
Pensions	Yes
Personal prop.	$7,500+
Tools	See pers. prop.
Business partn.	No

Ohio
Homestead	$5,000
Vehicle	$1,000
Annuity/Ins.	Yes
Pensions	Yes
Personal prop.	$1,500+
Tools	$750
Business partn.	Yes

Oklahoma
Homestead	Unlimited
Vehicle	$3,000
Annuity/Ins.	Yes
Pensions	Yes
Personal prop.	$4,000+
Tools	$5,000
Business partn.	Yes

Oregon
Homestead	$25,000
Vehicle	$1,700
Annuity/Ins.	Yes
Pensions	Yes
Personal prop.	$7,500+
Tools	$3,000
Business partn.	No

Pennsylvania
Homestead	None
Vehicle	-
Annuity/Ins.	Yes
Pensions	Yes
Personal prop.	$300+
Tools	Sewing mach.
Business partn.	Yes

Rhode Island
Homestead	$150,000
Vehicle	$10,000
Annuity/Ins.	Yes
Pensions	Yes
Personal prop.	$8,600+
Tools	41,200
Business partn.	Yes

South Carolina
Homestead	$5,000
Vehicle	$1,200
Annuity/Ins.	Yes
Pensions	Yes
Personal prop.	$2,500+
Tools	$750
Business partn.	Yes

South Dakota

Homestead	Unlimited
Vehicle	See pers. prop.
Annuity/Ins.	Yes
Pensions	Yes
Personal prop.	$4,000+
Tools	No
Business partn.	No

Tennessee

Homestead	$5,000
Vehicle	See pers. prop.
Annuity/Ins.	Yes
Pensions	Yes
Personal prop.	$4,000+
Tools	$1,900
Business partn.	Yes

Texas

Homestead	Unlimited
Vehicle	See pers. prop.
Annuity/Ins.	Yes
Pensions	Yes
Personal prop.	$30,000
Tools	See pers. prop.
Business partn.	Yes

Utah

Homestead	$20,000
Vehicle	Yes
Annuity/Ins.	Yes
Pensions	Yes
Personal prop.	$1,500+
Tools	$3,500
Business partn.	Yes

Vermont

Homestead	$75,000
Vehicle	$2,500
Annuity/Ins.	Yes
Pensions	Yes
Personal prop.	$7,000+
Tools	$5,000
Business partn.	No

Virginia

Homestead	$5,000
Vehicle	$2,000
Annuity/Ins.	Yes
Pensions	Yes
Personal prop.	$5,000+
Tools	$10,000
Business partn.	Yes

Washington

Homestead	$40,000
Vehicle	$2,500
Annuity/Ins.	Yes
Pensions	Yes
Personal prop.	$2,700+
Tools	$5,000
Business partn.	Yes

West Virginia

Homestead	$25,000
Vehicle	$2,400
Annuity/Ins.	Yes
Pensions	Yes
Personal prop.	$8,000+
Tools	$1,500
Business partn.	Yes

Wisconsin

Homestead	$40,000
Vehicle	$1,200
Annuity/Ins.	Yes
Pensions	Yes
Personal prop.	$5,000+
Tools	$7,500
Business partn.	Yes

Wyoming

Homestead	$10,000
Vehicle	$2,400
Annuity/Ins.	Yes
Pensions	Yes
Personal prop.	$2,000+
Tools	$2,000
Business partn.	No

B Forms

As explained in this manual, there are several simple things you can do to protect yourself from lawsuits. Some of these require using certain legal language or forms in your affairs.

This appendix contains some of the most useful forms you can use in protecting yourself from claims. The forms and their uses are as follows:

Form 1: Addendum to Contract Attach this addendum to every contract you sign. It says that any dispute between the parties will be handled through arbitration, rather than in court. It will save you much time and a fortune in legal fees, unless, of course your spouse or child is a lawyer. In such a case you would probably rather go to court.

Form 2: Employment Contract 1 Use this agreement whenever you or a company you own hires an employee. It is meant to protect you from charges of discrimination sexual harassment, labor violations and other such charges.

Form 3: Employment Contract 2 This is a similar employment agreement but leaves out the trade secret and noncompete clauses. Employment contract 1 is better, and you should use it whenever possible, but if you do not want to be as harsh but still want to have some protections, use this contract.

Form 4: IRS Form SS-8 This form is used to determine if a person you treat as an independent contractor actually qualifies as such.

Forms 5 & 6: Tenancy by the Entireties Assignments 1 and 2 In states where tenancy by the entireties property is exempt from creditors, these forms will make property you own jointly with your spouse safe from claims by creditors against one of you. Use Part 1 to convey property owned by spouses separately and together to a third person such as a child or parent. Immediately thereafter have that person use Part 2 to convey it back to the spouses in an estate by the entireties.

Form 7: State Exemptions Worksheet Use this form to analyze your state's exemptions and whether what you own is exempt.

Addendum to Contract

This Addendum is made to that contract dated_____, 200_____, between
_____ and _____
_____ as follows:

    ARBITRATION. In the event a dispute of any nature arises between the parties to the contract, the parties hereto agree to submit the dispute to binding arbitration in _____ County, State of _____ under the rules of the American Arbitration Association.

    An award rendered by the arbitrator(s) shall be final and binding upon the parties and judgment on such award may be entered by either party in the highest court having jurisdiction.

    Each party hereto specifically waives his or her right to bring the dispute before a court of law and stipulates that this agreement shall be a complete defense to any action instituted in any local, state or federal court or before any administrative tribunal.

_____   _____

_____   _____

_____   _____

Employment Contract

Employer, _____ agrees to employ _____ as employee and employee agrees to work for employer under the following terms and conditions:

Term. Either party is free to terminate this relationship at any time. Employee may resign at any time and for any reason and employer may terminate employee at any time and for any reason.

Duties. Employee is employed in the position of _____ to serve and perform such duties at such times and places and in such manner as employer may from time to time direct. Employee agrees to perform such duties to the best of his or her ability, to devote his or her ability, to devote full and undivided time during working hours to the employer's business, to remit promptly to employer all money or property belonging to employer, and to not engage in any activity in competition with employer's business.

Compensation. Employee shall initially be paid the sum of _____ per _____ as full payment for services performed for employer. This sum may be raised or lowered by agreement of the parties based upon the performance of the employee.

Probation. It is understood between the parties that the first _____ days of employment shall be probationary only and that if employee's services are not satisfactory to employer employment shall be terminated at the end of this probationary period.

Law. It is employer's intention to comply with all federal, state and local laws which apply to the business, including labor, equal opportunity, privacy and sexual harassment. Employee shall promptly report any violations encountered in the business. Employee shall at all times comply with any and all federal, state and local laws.

Trade Secrets. Employee understands that as part of the employment he or she will have access to confidential information of the employer and may participate in developing such information as part of the employment duties. Employee acknowledges that such information contains the valuable trade secrets of the employer. Employee agrees to at no time disclose them to anyone other than authorized employees, and to not remove from the premises any equipment or information without the consent of employer. Trade secrets of employer include but are not limited to customer lists, terms of payment, suppliers, methods, processes, or marketing plans.

Contracts. Employee shall not have the power to make any contracts or commitments on behalf of employer without express written consent of employer.

Noncompete. Employee agrees not to compete with employer's business for a term of _____ years in a radius of _____ miles from employer's business.

Waiver. In the event one party fails to insist upon performance of a part this agreement, such failure shall not be construed as waiving those terms and this entire agreement shall remain in full force

Arbitration. In the event a dispute of any nature arises between the parties to the contract, the parties hereto agree to submit the dispute to binding arbitration under the rules of the American Arbitration Association. An award rendered by the arbitrator(s) shall be final and binding upon the parties and judgment on such award may be entered by either party in the highest court having jurisdiction. Each party hereto specifically waives his or her right to bring the dispute before a court of law and stipulates that this agreement shall be a complete defense to any action instituted in any local, state or federal court or before any administrative tribunal.

Entire agreement. The parties agree that this document embodies the entire agreement between the parties and that no other oral or written representations or warranties have been made.

Reasonableness. Employee has read this contract and agrees that all clauses herein are reasonable to protect employer's business.

Severability. In the event any part of this agreement is found to be illegal, unenforceable, or against public policy, the parties agree that such part shall be modified or deleted so as to make this agreement enforceable.

In witness whereof, the parties have executed this agreement this ____ day of _____, 200____.

Employer: _____ Employee:

By:_____ _____

Employment Contract

Employer, _____, agrees to employ _____ as employee, and employee agrees to work for employer under the following terms and conditions:

Term. Either party is free to terminate this relationship at any time. Employee may resign at any time and for any reason and employer may terminate employee at any time and for any reason.

Duties. Employee is employed in the position of _____ to serve and perform such duties at such times and places and in such manner as employer may from time to time direct. Employee agrees to perform such duties to the best of his or her ability, to devote his or her ability, to devote full and undivided time during working hours to the employer's business, to remit promptly to employer all money or property belonging to employer, and to not engage in any activity in competition with employer's business.

Compensation. Employee shall initially be paid the sum of _____ per _____ as full payment for services performed for employer. This sum may be raised or lowered by agreement of the parties based upon the performance of the employee.

Probation. It is understood between the parties that the first _____ days of employment shall be probationary only and that if employee's services are not satisfactory to employer employment shall be terminated at the end of this probationary period.

Law. It is employer's intention to comply with all federal, state and local laws which apply to the business, including labor, equal opportunity, privacy and sexual harassment. Employee shall promptly report any violations encountered in the business. Employee shall at all times comply with any and all federal, state and local laws.

Waiver. In the event one party fails to insist upon performance of a part this agreement, such failure shall not be construed as waiving those terms and this entire agreement shall remain in full force

Arbitration. In the event a dispute of any nature arises between the parties to the contract, the parties hereto agree to submit the dispute to binding arbitration under the rules of the American Arbitration Association. An award rendered by the arbitrator(s) shall be final and binding upon the parties and judgment on such award may be entered by either party in the highest court having jurisdiction. Each party hereto specifically waives his or her right to bring the dispute before a court of law and stipulates that this agreement shall be a complete defense to any action instituted in any local, state or federal court or before any administrative tribunal.

Entire agreement. The parties agree that this document embodies the entire agreement between the parties and that no other oral or written representations or warranties have been made.

Severability. In the event any part of this agreement is found to be illegal, unenforceable, or against public policy, the parties agree that such part shall be modified or deleted so as to make this agreement enforceable.

In witness whereof, the parties have executed this agreement this ____ day of _____, 200___.

Employer: _____ Employee:

By:_____ _____

Form **SS-8**
(Rev. January 2001)
Department of the Treasury
Internal Revenue Service

Determination of Worker Status for Purposes of Federal Employment Taxes and Income Tax Withholding

OMB No. 1545-0004

Name of firm (or person) for whom the worker performed services

Worker's name

Firm's address (include street address, apt. or suite no., city, state, and ZIP code)

Worker's address (include street address, apt. or suite no., city, state, and ZIP code)

Trade name

Telephone number (include area code)
( )

Worker's social security number

Telephone number (include area code)
( )

Firm's employer identification number

Worker's employer identification number (if any)

Important Information Needed To Process Your Request

If this form is being completed by the worker, the IRS must have your permission to disclose your name to the firm. Do you object to disclosing your name and the information on this form to the firm? . . . . ☐ Yes ☐ No
If you answered "Yes" or did not check a box, stop here. The IRS cannot act on your request and a determination will not be issued.

You must answer ALL items OR mark them "Unknown" or "Does not apply." If you need more space, attach another sheet.

A This form is being completed by: ☐ Firm ☐ Worker; for services performed _____ to _____ .
  (beginning date) (ending date)

B Explain your reason(s) for filing this form (e.g., you received a bill from the IRS, you believe you received a Form 1099 or Form W-2 erroneously, you are unable to get worker's compensation benefits, you were audited or are being audited by the IRS). ....
....
....
....

C Total number of workers who performed or are performing the same or similar services _____ .

D How did the worker obtain the job? ☐ Application ☐ Bid ☐ Employment Agency ☐ Other (specify) _____

E Attach copies of all supporting documentation (contracts, invoices, memos, Forms W-2, Forms 1099, IRS closing agreements, IRS rulings, etc.). In addition, please inform us of any current or past litigation concerning the worker's status. If no income reporting forms (Form 1099-MISC or W-2) were furnished to the worker, enter the amount of income earned for the year(s) at issue $ _____ .

F Describe the firm's business. ....
....
....
....
....

G Describe the work done by the worker and provide the worker's job title. ....
....
....
....

H Explain why you believe the worker is an employee or an independent contractor. ....
....
....
....

I Did the worker perform services for the firm before getting this position? . . . . ☐ Yes ☐ No ☐ N/A
 If "Yes," what were the dates of the prior service? ....
 If "Yes," explain the differences, if any, between the current and prior service. ....
....
....
....

J If the work is done under a written agreement between the firm and the worker, attach a copy (preferably signed by both parties). Describe the terms and conditions of the work arrangement. ....

For Privacy Act and Paperwork Reduction Act Notice, see page 5.   Cat. No. 16106T   Form **SS-8** (Rev. 1-2001)

Form SS-8 (Rev. 1-2001) Page **2**

Part I Behavioral Control

1. What specific training and/or instruction is the worker given by the firm? ....
2. How does the worker receive work assignments? ....
3. Who determines the methods by which the assignments are performed? ....
4. Who is the worker required to contact if problems or complaints arise and who is responsible for their resolution? ....
5. What types of reports are required from the worker? Attach examples. ....
6. Describe the worker's daily routine (i.e., schedule, hours, etc.). ....
7. At what location(s) does the worker perform services (e.g., firm's premises, own shop or office, home, customer's location, etc.)? ....
8. Describe any meetings the worker is required to attend and any penalties for not attending (e.g., sales meetings, monthly meetings, staff meetings, etc.). ....
9. Is the worker required to provide the services personally? ☐ Yes ☐ No
10. If substitutes or helpers are needed, who hires them? ....
11. If the worker hires the substitutes or helpers, is approval required? ☐ Yes ☐ No
    If "Yes," by whom? ....
12. Who pays the substitutes or helpers? ....
13. Is the worker reimbursed if the worker pays the substitutes or helpers? ☐ Yes ☐ No
    If "Yes," by whom? ....

Part II Financial Control

1. List the supplies, equipment, materials, and property provided by each party:
   The firm ....
   The worker ....
   Other party ....
2. Does the worker lease equipment? ☐ Yes ☐ No
   If "Yes," what are the terms of the lease? (Attach a copy or explanatory statement.) ....
3. What expenses are incurred by the worker in the performance of services for the firm? ....
4. Specify which, if any, expenses are reimbursed by:
   The firm ....
   Other party ....
5. Type of pay the worker receives: ☐ Salary ☐ Commission ☐ Hourly Wage ☐ Piece Work
   ☐ Lump Sum ☐ Other (specify) ....
   If type of pay is commission, and the firm guarantees a minimum amount of pay, specify amount $ _____ .
6. If the worker is paid by a firm other than the one listed on this form for these services, enter name, address, and employer identification number of the payer. ....
7. Is the worker allowed a drawing account for advances? ☐ Yes ☐ No
   If "Yes," how often? ....
   Specify any restrictions. ....
8. Whom does the customer pay? ☐ Firm ☐ Worker
   If worker, does the worker pay the total amount to the firm? ☐ Yes ☐ No If "No," explain. ....
9. Does the firm carry worker's compensation insurance on the worker? ☐ Yes ☐ No
10. What economic loss or financial risk, if any, can the worker incur beyond the normal loss of salary (e.g., loss or damage of equipment, material, etc.)? ....

Form **SS-8** (Rev. 1-2001)

Form SS-8 (Rev. 1-2001) Page **3**

Part III — Relationship of the Worker and Firm

1. List the benefits available to the worker (e.g., paid vacations, sick pay, pensions, bonuses). ....
2. Can the relationship be terminated by either party without incurring liability or penalty? .... ☐ Yes ☐ No
   If "No," explain your answer. ....
3. Does the worker perform similar services for others? .... ☐ Yes ☐ No
   If "Yes," is the worker required to get approval from the firm? .... ☐ Yes ☐ No
4. Describe any agreements prohibiting competition between the worker and the firm while the worker is performing services or during any later period. Attach any available documentation. ....
5. Is the worker a member of a union? .... ☐ Yes ☐ No
6. What type of advertising, if any, does the worker do (e.g., a business listing in a directory, business cards, etc.)? Provide copies, if applicable. ....
7. If the worker assembles or processes a product at home, who provides the materials and instructions or pattern? ....
8. What does the worker do with the finished product (e.g., return it to the firm, provide it to another party, or sell it)? ....
9. How does the firm represent the worker to its customers (e.g., employee, partner, representative, or contractor)? ....
10. If the worker no longer performs services for the firm, how did the relationship end? ....

Part IV — For Service Providers or Salespersons

Complete this part if the worker provided a service directly to customers or is a salesperson.

1. What are the worker's responsibilities in soliciting new customers? ....
2. Who provides the worker with leads to prospective customers? ....
3. Describe any reporting requirements pertaining to the leads. ....
4. What terms and conditions of sale, if any, are required by the firm? ....
5. Are orders submitted to and subject to approval by the firm? .... ☐ Yes ☐ No
6. Who determines the worker's territory? ....
7. Did the worker pay for the privilege of serving customers on the route or in the territory? .... ☐ Yes ☐ No
   If "Yes," whom did the worker pay? ....
   If "Yes," how much did the worker pay? .... $ _____
8. Where does the worker sell the product (e.g., in a home, retail establishment, etc.)? ....
9. List the product and/or services distributed by the worker (e.g., meat, vegetables, fruit, bakery products, beverages, or laundry or dry cleaning services). If more than one type of product and/or service is distributed, specify the principal one. ....
10. Does the worker sell life insurance full time? .... ☐ Yes ☐ No
11. Does the worker sell other types of insurance for the firm? .... ☐ Yes ☐ No
    If "Yes," enter the percentage of the worker's total working time spent in selling other types of insurance. .... _____%
12. If the worker solicits orders from wholesalers, retailers, contractors, or operators of hotels, restaurants, or other similar establishments, enter the percentage of the worker's time spent in the solicitation. .... _____%
13. Is the merchandise purchased by the customers for resale or use in their business operations? .... ☐ Yes ☐ No
    Describe the merchandise and state whether it is equipment installed on the customers' premises. ....

Part V — Signature (see page 4)

Under penalties of perjury, I declare that I have examined this request, including accompanying documents, and to the best of my knowledge and belief, the facts presented are true, correct, and complete.

Signature ▶ _____ Title ▶ _____ Date ▶ _____
(Type or print name below)

Form **SS-8** (Rev. 1-2001)

General Instructions

Section references are to the Internal Revenue Code unless otherwise noted.

Purpose

Firms and workers file Form SS-8 to request a determination of the status of a worker for purposes of Federal employment taxes and income tax withholding.

A Form SS-8 determination may be requested only in order to resolve Federal tax matters. The taxpayer requesting a determination must file an income tax return for the years under consideration before a determination can be issued. If Form SS-8 is submitted for a tax year for which the statute of limitations on the tax return has expired, a determination letter will not be issued. The statute of limitations expires 3 years from the due date of the tax return or the date filed, whichever is later.

The IRS does not issue a determination letter for proposed transactions or on hypothetical situations. We may, however, issue an information letter when it is considered appropriate.

Definition

Firm. For the purposes of this form, the term "firm" means any individual, business enterprise, organization, state, or other entity for which a worker has performed services. The firm may or may not have paid the worker directly for these services. **If the firm was not responsible for payment for services, please be sure to complete question 6 in Part II of Form SS-8.**

The SS-8 Determination Process

The IRS will acknowledge the receipt of your Form SS-8. Because there are usually two (or more) parties who could be affected by a determination of employment status, the IRS attempts to get information from all parties involved by sending those parties blank Forms SS-8 for completion. The case will be assigned to a technician who will review the facts, apply the law, and render a decision. The technician may ask for additional information before rendering a decision. The IRS will generally issue a formal determination to the firm or payer (if that is a different entity), and will send a copy to the worker. A determination letter applies only to a worker (or a class of workers) requesting it, and the decision is binding on the IRS. In certain cases, a formal determination will not be issued; instead, an information letter may be issued. Although an information letter is advisory only and is not binding on the IRS, it may be used to assist the worker to fulfill his or her Federal tax obligations. This process takes approximately 120 days.

Neither the SS-8 determination process nor the review of any records in connection with the determination constitutes an examination (audit) of any Federal tax return. If the periods under consideration have previously been examined, the SS-8 determination process will not constitute a reexamination under IRS reopening procedures. Because this is not an examination of any Federal tax return, the appeal rights available in connection with an examination do not apply to an SS-8 determination. However, if you disagree with a determination and you have additional information concerning the work relationship that you believe was not previously considered, you may request that the determining office reconsider the determination.

Completing Form SS-8

Please answer all questions as completely as possible. Attach additional sheets if you need more space. Provide information for all years the worker provided services for the firm. Determinations are based on the entire relationship between the firm and the worker.

Additional copies of this form may be obtained by calling 1-800-TAX-FORM (1-800-829-3676) or from the IRS Web Site at **www.irs.gov**.

Fee

There is no fee for requesting an SS-8 determination letter.

Signature

The Form SS-8 must be signed and dated by the taxpayer. A stamped signature will not be accepted.

The person who signs for a corporation must be an officer of the corporation who has personal knowledge of the facts. If the corporation is a member of an affiliated group filing a consolidated return, it must be signed by an officer of the common parent of the group.

The person signing for a trust, partnership, or limited liability company must be, respectively, a trustee, general partner, or member-manager who has personal knowledge of the facts.

Where To File

Send the completed Form SS-8 to the address listed below for the firm's location. However, for cases involving Federal agencies, send the form to the Internal Revenue Service, Attn: CC:CORP:T:C, Ben Franklin Station, P.O. Box 7604, Washington, DC 20044.

Firm's location:	Send to:
Alaska, Arizona, Arkansas, California, Colorado, Hawaii, Idaho, Illinois, Iowa, Kansas, Minnesota, Missouri, Montana, Nebraska, Nevada, New Mexico, North Dakota, Oklahoma, Oregon, South Dakota, Texas, Utah, Washington, Wisconsin, Wyoming, American Samoa, Guam, Puerto Rico, U.S. Virgin Islands	Internal Revenue Service SS-8 Determinations P.O. Box 1231 Stop 4106 AUCSC Austin, TX 78767
Alabama, Connecticut, Delaware, District of Columbia, Florida, Georgia, Indiana, Kentucky, Louisiana, Maine, Maryland, Massachusetts, Michigan, Mississippi, New Hampshire, New Jersey, New York, North Carolina, Ohio, Pennsylvania, Rhode Island, South Carolina, Tennessee, Vermont, Virginia, West Virginia, all other locations not listed	Internal Revenue Service SS-8 Determinations 40 Lakemont Road Newport, VT 05855-1555

Instructions for Workers

If you are requesting a determination for more than one firm, complete a separate Form SS-8 for each firm.

 Form SS-8 is not a claim for refund of social security and Medicare taxes or Federal income tax withholding.

If you are found to be an employee, you are responsible for filing an amended return for any corrections related to this decision. A determination that a worker is an employee does not necessarily reduce any current or prior tax liability. For more information, call 1-800-829-1040.

Form SS-8 (Rev. 1-2001) Page **5**

Time for filing a claim for refund. Generally, you must file your claim for a credit or refund within 3 years from the date your original return was filed or within 2 years from the date the tax was paid, whichever is later.

Form SS-8 does not prevent the expiration of the time in which a claim for a refund must be filed. If you are concerned about a refund, and the statute of limitations for filing a claim for refund for the year(s) at issue has not yet expired, you should file **Form 1040X,** Amended U.S. Individual Income Tax Return, to protect your statute of limitations. File a separate Form 1040X for each year.

On the Form 1040X you file, do not complete lines 1 through 24 on the form. Write "Protective Claim" at the top of the form, sign and date it. In addition, you should enter the following statement in Part II, Explanation of Changes to Income, Deductions, and Credits: "Filed Form SS-8 with the Internal Revenue Service Office in (Austin, TX; Newport, VT; or Washington, DC; as appropriate). By filing this protective claim, I reserve the right to file a claim for any refund that may be due after a determination of my employment tax status has been completed."

Filing Form SS-8 does not alter the requirement to timely file an income tax return. Do not delay filing your tax return in anticipation of an answer to your SS-8 request. You must file an income tax return for related tax years before a determination can be issued. In addition, if applicable, do not delay in responding to a request for payment while waiting for a determination of your worker status.

Instructions for Firms

If a **worker** has requested a determination of his or her status while working for you, you will receive a request from the IRS to complete a Form SS-8. In cases of this type, the IRS usually gives each party an opportunity to present a statement of the facts because any decision will affect the employment tax status of the parties. Failure to respond to this request will not prevent the IRS from issuing an information letter to the worker based on the information he or she has made available so that the worker may fulfill his or her Federal tax obligations. However, the information that you provide is extremely valuable in determining the status of the worker.

If **you** are requesting a determination for a particular class of worker, complete the form for **one** individual who is representative of the class of workers whose status is in question. If you want a written determination for more than one class of workers, complete a separate Form SS-8 for one worker from each class whose status is typical of that class. A written determination for any worker will apply to other workers of the same class if the facts are not materially different for these workers. Please provide a list of names and addresses of all workers potentially affected by this determination.

If you have a reasonable basis for not treating a worker as an employee, you may be relieved from having to pay employment taxes for that worker under section 530 of the 1978 Revenue Act. However, this relief provision cannot be considered in conjunction with a Form SS-8 determination because the determination does not constitute an examination of any tax return. For more information regarding section 530 of the 1978 Revenue Act and to determine if you qualify for relief under this section, you may visit the IRS Web Site at **www.irs.gov**.

Privacy Act and Paperwork Reduction Act Notice. We ask for the information on this form to carry out the Internal Revenue laws of the United States. This information will be used to determine the employment status of the worker(s) described on the form. Subtitle C, Employment Taxes, of the Internal Revenue Code imposes employment taxes on wages. Sections 3121(d), 3306(a), and 3401(c) and (d) and the related regulations define employee and employer for purposes of employment taxes imposed under Subtitle C. Section 6001 authorizes the IRS to request information needed to determine if a worker(s) or firm is subject to these taxes. Section 6109 requires you to provide your taxpayer identification number. Neither workers nor firms are required to request a status determination, but if you choose to do so, you must provide the information requested on this form. Failure to provide the requested information may prevent us from making a status determination. If any worker or the firm has requested a status determination, and you are being asked to provide information for use in that determination, you are not required to provide the requested information. However, failure to provide such information will prevent the IRS from considering it in making the status determination. Providing false or fraudulent information may subject you to penalties. Routine uses of this information include providing it to the Department of Justice for use in civil and criminal litigation, to the Social Security Administration for the administration of social security programs, and to cities, states, and the District of Columbia for the administration of their tax laws. We may also provide this information to the affected worker(s) or the firm as part of the status determination process.

You are not required to provide the information requested on a form that is subject to the Paperwork Reduction Act unless the form displays a valid OMB control number. Books or records relating to a form or its instructions must be retained as long as their contents may become material in the administration of any Internal Revenue law. Generally, tax returns and return information are confidential, as required by section 6103.

The time needed to complete and file this form will vary depending on individual circumstances. The estimated average time is: **Recordkeeping,** 22 hrs.; **Learning about the law or the form,** 47 min.; and **Preparing and sending the form to the IRS,** 1 hr., 11 min. If you have comments concerning the accuracy of these time estimates or suggestions for making this form simpler, we would be happy to hear from you. You can write to the Tax Forms Committee, Western Area Distribution Center, Rancho Cordova, CA 95743-0001. **Do not** send the tax form to this address. Instead, see **Where To File** on page 4.

Assignment

Date:_____, 200___

    The undersigned, _____ in consideration of the sum of one dollar, receipt of which is acknowledged, and other good and valuable consideration, hereby assign, transfer and deliver to _____, the following personal property:

Assignors: Assignee:

_____   _____

_____

Assignment
Tenancy by the Entireties

Date:_____, 200___

    The undersigned, _____ in consideration of the sum of one dollar, receipt of which is acknowledged, and other good and valuable consideration, hereby assign, transfer and deliver to _____and_____ _____, husband and wife, in an estate by the entireties, the following personal property:

Assignor: Assignees:

_____   _____

                                                                                                        _____

State Exemptions Worksheet

Homestead: $_____
Requirements & Limitations: _____
_____
_____

Tenancy by the entireties safe from creditors? _____
Tenancy by the entireties applies to personal property? _____

Pensions: $ _____
Restrictions: _____
_____
_____

Annuities: $ _____
Restrictions: _____
_____
_____

Insurance: $ _____
Restrictions: _____
_____
_____

Wages: $ _____
Restrictions: _____
_____
_____

Tools of Trade: $ _____
Restrictions: _____
_____
_____

Other: $ _____
Restrictions: _____
_____
_____
_____
_____

Index

A-B trusts, 164
Accidents, 16
Acts of others, 17
AFDC, 135
Aircraft, 76
Alimony, 31, 133, 214
Annuities, 123
Annunzio-Wylie Act of 1992, 83
Anti-drug Abuse Act of 1988, 82
Arbitration, 55
Asset protection trusts, 171

Badges of fraud, 26
Bank Secrecy Act of 1970, 81
Bankruptcy reform, 206
Bankruptcy, 29, 36, 139, 199
Beneficiary, 34
Boats, 76
Bulletproof asset protection, 24
Burial plots, 137
Business contracts, 57
Business trust, 53, 187

Cash, 70
Changing your name, 79
Chapter 11 bankruptcy, 36
Chapter 13 bankruptcy, 36, 201
Chapter 20 bankruptcy, 36

Chapter 7 bankruptcy, 36, 201
Charging order, 35
Charitable remainder trusts, 169
Checking accounts, 73
Child support, 31, 133
Children, 147
Children's trusts, 165
Claimant, 33
Collectibles, 76
College investment plans, 137
Community property, 106
Constructive fraud, 27
Consumer credit protection act, 118
Contempt of court, 33, 34
Contingent fees, 11
Converting assets, 87
Corporation, 34, 48, 75
Costs of asset protection, 41
CRAT, 170
Credit cards, 72
Creditor, 33
Criminal laws, 80
CRU, 170

Debtor, 33
Debts, 15
Defendant, 33
Deposition, 34

Destroying records, 80
Directors, 35
Discharge in bankruptcy, 205
Divorce, 18, 116, 214
Docketing, 34
Domestic asset protection trusts, 171
Drunk driving, 31

Employees, 47, 57
Enjoying your assets, 217
Equity stripping, 93
ERISA, 113
Evaluating your exposure, 219
Exempt property, 34
Exemptions, 85, 221

Financial statement, 65
Financing a sale, 62
Foundations, 190
Fraud, 31, 34
Fraudulent conveyance, 36
Fraudulent transfer laws, 26
Future acquisitions, 95

Garnishment, 34
General partners, 35
General partnerships, 155
Gifts, 143
Giving security, 200
Gold, 76
Grantor, 34
GRIT, 102

Hiding assets, 207
Hiding yourself, 211
Holder in due course, 62
Homestead, 34, 93, 97

Independent contractors, 58
Insulating from transactions, 61
Insurance, 45, 119
Intent, 25, 140
IRAs, 114
Irrevocable life insurance trust, 121
Irrevocable trust, 53, 164
Joint and severable liability, 17
Joint tenancy, 105
Jurisdiction, 56

Keogh plan, 114

Land trust, 53, 75
Leases, 59
Legal entities, 47
Legal research, 223
Legal violations, 16
Levy, 34
Life insurance, 119
Limited liability company, 34, 51, 76, 149
Limited partners, 35
Limited partnership, 34, 52, 76, 157
Liquor licenses, 137
Living trust, 53, 75, 163

Marital agreements, 59
Mediation, 56
Members, 35
Money Laundering Control act of 1986, 82
Money Laund. Suppression Act of 1994, 82

Nondischargeable debts, 31
Nonprofit corporations, 189
Non-qualified plans, 114

Officers, 35
Offshore annuities, 125
Offshore LLCs, 152
Offshore trusts, 175

Pensions, 113
Perjury, 34
Personal property, 131
Plaintiff, 33
Premarital agreements, 59
Privacy, 65
Private annuities, 125
Public benefits, 135

Radon gas, 60
Real estate contracts, 59
Real estate, 74
Receivables, 126
Retirement accounts, 113
Risks, 43
Roth IRAs, 115

Settling a case, 197
Settlor, 34
Shareholders, 35
Shielding yourself against claims, 43
Shifting property, 139
Social security, 133

Spendthrift trust, 35, 171
State shopping, 91
Statutes of limitation, 19, 31
Stopping creditors, 200
Subpoena, 34, 65

Tenancy in common, 105
Tenants by the entireties, 34, 102, 105
Tools of trade, 129
Trust, 34, 52, 163-188
Trustee, 34

Uniform Fraudulent Conveyances Act, 26
Uniform Fraudulent Transfer Act, 26
USA PATRIOT Act of 2001, 83

Venue, 56
Volunteering, 43

Wages, 117
Wrongful acts, 16

Other Self-Help Law Books by Mark Warda

National Titles
- ☐ **Land Trusts** for Privacy & Profit (national ed.) 34.95
- ☐ **Land Trusts** for Privacy & Profit Forms only on CD 14.95
- ☐ How to Register Your Own **Copyright** (3rd ed.) 21.95
- ☐ How to Register Your Own **Trademark** (3rd ed.) 21.95
- ☐ Essential Guide to Real Estate **Contracts** 18.95
- ☐ Essential Guide to Real Estate **Leases** 18.95
- ☐ **Neighbor** vs. **Neighbor** (2nd ed.) 16.95
- ☐ How to Form Your Own **Corporation** (3rd ed.) 24.95
- ☐ How to Form a **Limited Liability Company** 22.95
- ☐ How to Form a **Nonprofit** Corporation 24.95
- ☐ Incorporate in **Delaware** from Any State 24.95
- ☐ How to form a **Nevada Corporation** from Any State 24.95
- ☐ How to Make Your Own **Simple Will** (3rd ed.) 16.95
- ☐ The Most Valuable **Personal Legal Forms** 19.95

Florida Titles
- ☐ **Landlords'** Rights and Duties in Florida (8th ed.) 21.95
- ☐ **Landlords'** Forms only on CD 14.95
- ☐ **Land Trusts** in Florida (6th ed.) 29.95
- ☐ **Land Trusts** in Florida Forms only on CD 14.95
- ☐ How to Form a **Florida Corporation** (5th ed.) 24.95
- ☐ How to Form an **LLC in Florida** (2nd ed.) 24.95
- ☐ How to **Start a Business** in Florida (6th ed.) 18.95
- ☐ How to Make a Florida **Will** (6th ed.) 16.95
- ☐ How to Win in **Small Claims Court** in Fla.(7th ed.) 18.95

California Titles
- ☐ **Landlords'** Legal Guide in California 24.95
- ☐ How to **Start a Business** in California 18.95
- ☐ How to Make a California **Will** 16.95
- ☐ How to Win in **Small Claims Court** in California. 18.95

Georgia Titles
- ☐ How to **Start a Business** in Georgia 21.95
- ☐ How to Make a **Georgia Will** 16.95

Illinois Titles
- ☐ **Landlords'** Legal Guide in **Illinois** 24.95
- ☐ How to **Start a Business** in **Illinois** 21.95
- ☐ How to Make Your own **Illinois Will** 16.95

Massachusetts Titles
- ☐ **Landlords'** Legal Guide in **Massachusetts** 24.95
- ☐ How to **Start a Business** in **Massachusetts** 21.95
- ☐ How to Make a **Massachusetts Will** 16.95
- ☐ How to Form a **Massachusetts Corporation** 24.95

Michigan Titles
- ☐ How to **Start a Business** in **Michigan** 18.95
- ☐ How to Make a **Michigan Will** 16.95

Minnesota Titles
- ☐ How to Make a **Minnesota Will** 16.95
- ☐ How to Form a **Minnesota Corporation** 24.95

New York Titles
- ☐ **Landlords'** Legal Guide in **New York** 24.95
- ☐ How to **Start a Business** in **New York** 18.95
- ☐ How to Make a **New York Will** 16.95
- ☐ How to Form a **New York Corporation** 24.95
- ☐ How to Win in **Small Claims Court** in N. Y. 18.95

North Carolina Titles
- ☐ **Landlords'** Legal Guide in **North Carolina** 24.95
- ☐ How to **Start a Business** in **North Carolina** 21.95
- ☐ How to Make a **North Carolina Will** 16.95

Ohio Titles
- ☐ How to Form a **Corporation in Ohio** 24.95
- ☐ How to Make an Ohio **Will** 16.95

Pennsylvania Titles
- ☐ **Landlords'** Legal Guide in **Pennsylvania** 24.95
- ☐ How to **Start a Business** in **Pennsylvania** 18.95
- ☐ How to Make a **Pennsylvania Will** 16.95

Texas Titles
- ☐ **Landlords'** Legal Guide in **Texas** 24.95
- ☐ How to **Start a Business** in **Texas** 18.95
- ☐ How to Make a **Texas Will** 16.95
- ☐ How to Form a **Texas Corporation** (5th ed.) 24.95
- ☐ How to Win in **Small Claims Court** in Texas (7th ed.) 16.95

You can order by mail (Galt Press, P. O. Box 8, Clearwater, FL 33757), by fax (727-585-8423), by phone (727-581-8685) or by email (galt@warda.net). If ordering by email, put half of your credit card number in each of 2 separate e-mails and include the expiration date with one of them. All orders must be prepaid. We accept Discover, MasterCard and Visa. New credit card processing rules require us to have your credit card billing zip code.

Credit Card No. _____ Exp. _____

Zip code on credit card billing address _____

Name _____

Address _____

City, State _____ Zip _____

Signature for credit card _____

Books total $_____

Florida sales tax _____

Shipping* _____

Total order $_____

*Shipping: Add $2.39 for book rate or $4.30 for priority mail per order (not per book).